LIFE AND LITERATURE OF THE SOUTHWEST

GUIDE TO
LIFE AND
LITERATURE OF
THE SOUTHWEST

REVISED AND ENLARGED
IN BOTH KNOWLEDGE AND WISDOM

J. FRANK DOBIE

SOUTHERN METHODIST UNIVERSITY PRESS · DALLAS

Not copyright in 1942

Again not copyright in 1952

Anybody is welcome to help himself to any
of it in any way

Second printing 1958

Third printing 1961

Fourth printing 1963

Fifth printing 1965

Sixth printing 1969

Seventh printing 1974

LIBRARY OF CONGRESS CATALOG CARD NUMBER: 52-11834

Over: "Indian Summer," by Will Crawford, from the
J. Frank Dobie Collection of Western Art.

Contents

Illustrations

A Preface With Some Revised Ideas

IT HAS BEEN ten years since I wrote the prefatory "Declaration" to this now enlarged and altered book. Not to my generation alone have many things receded during that decade. To the intelligent young as well as to the intelligent elderly, efforts in the present atmosphere to opiate the public with mere pictures of frontier enterprise have a ghastly unreality. The Texas Rangers have come to seem as remote as the Foreign Legion in France fighting against the Kaiser. Yet this *Guide,* extensively added to and revised, is mainly concerned, apart from the land and its native life, with frontier backgrounds. If during a decade a man does not change his mind on some things and develop new points of view, it is a pretty good sign that his mind is petrified and need no longer be accounted among the living. I have an inclination to rewrite the "Declaration," but maybe I was just as wise on some matters ten years ago as I am now; so I let it stand.

> Do I contradict myself?
> Very well then I contradict myself.

I have heard so much silly bragging by Texans that I now think it would be a blessing to themselves — and a relief to others — if the braggers did not know they lived in Texas. Yet the time is not likely to come when a human being will not be better adapted to his environments by knowing their nature; on the other hand, to study a provincial setting from a provincial point of view is restricting. Nobody should specialize on provincial writings before he has the perspective that only a good deal of good literature and wide history can give. I think it more important that a dweller in the

1

Southwest read *The Trial and Death of Socrates* than all the books extant on killings by Billy the Kid. I think this dweller will fit his land better by understanding Thomas Jefferson's oath ("I have sworn upon the altar of God eternal hostility against every form of tyranny over the mind of man") than by reading all the books that have been written on ranch lands and people. For any dweller of the Southwest who would have the land soak into him, Wordsworth's "Tintern Abbey," "Ode: Intimations of Immortality," "The Solitary Reaper," "Expostulation and Reply," and a few other poems are more conducive to a "wise passiveness" than any native writing.

There are no substitutes for nobility, beauty, and wisdom. One of the chief impediments to amplitude and intellectual freedom is provincial inbreeding. I am sorry to see writings of the Southwest substituted for noble and beautiful and wise literature to which all people everywhere are inheritors. When I began teaching "Life and Literature of the Southwest" I did not regard these writings as a substitute. To reread most of them would be boresome, though *Hamlet*, Boswell's *Johnson*, Lamb's *Essays*, and other genuine literature remain as quickening as ever.

Very likely I shall not teach the course again. I am positive I shall never revise this *Guide* again. It is in nowise a bibliography. I have made more additions to the "Range Life" chapter than to any other. I am a collector of such books. A collector is a person who gathers unto himself the worthless as well as the worthy. Since I did not make a nickel out of the original printing of the *Guide* and hardly expect to make enough to buy a California "ranch" out of the present printing, I have added several items, with accompanying remarks, more for my own pleasure than for benefit to society.

Were the listings halved, made more selective, the book might serve its purpose better. Anybody who wants to can slice it in any manner he pleases. I am as much against forced literary swallowings as I am against prohibitions on free tasting, chewing, and digestion. I rate censors, particularly those of church and state, as low as I rate character assassins; they often run together.

I'd like to make a book on *Emancipators of the Human Mind* — Emerson, Jefferson, Thoreau, Tom Paine, Newton, Arnold, Voltaire, Goethe. . . . When I reflect how few writings connected with the wide open spaces of the West and Southwest are wide enough to enter into such a volume, I realize acutely how desirable is perspective in patriotism.

Hundreds of the books listed in this *Guide* have given me pleasure as well as particles for the mosaic work of my own books; but, with minor exceptions, they increasingly seem to me to explore only the exteriors of life. There is in them much good humor but scant wit. The hunger for something afar is absent or battened down. Drought blasts the turf, but its unhealing blast to human hope is glossed over. The body's thirst for water is a recurring theme, but human thirst for love and just thinking is beyond consideration. Horses run with their riders to death or victory, but fleeting beauty haunts no soul to the "doorway of the dead." The land is often pictured as lonely, but the lone way of a human being's essential self is not for this extravert world. The banners of individualism are carried high, but the higher individualism that grows out of long looking for meanings in the human drama is negligible. Somebody is always riding around or into a "feudal domain." Nobody at all penetrates it or penetrates democracy with the wisdom that came to Lincoln in his loneliness: "As I would not be a *slave*, so I would not be a *master*. This expresses my idea of democracy. Whatever differs from this, to the extent of the difference, is no democracy." The mountains, the caves, the forests, the deserts have had no prophets to interpret either their silences or their voices. In short, these books are mostly only the stuff of literature, not literature itself, not the very stuff of life, not the distillations of mankind's "agony and bloody sweat."

An ignorant person attaches more importance to the chatter of small voices around him than to the noble language of remote individuals. The more he listens to the small, the smaller he grows. The hope of regional literature lies in outgrowing regionalism itself. On November 11, 1949, I gave a talk to the Texas Institute of Letters that was published in the Spring 1950 issue of the *Southwest Review*. The paragraphs that follow are taken therefrom.

Good writing about any region is good only to the extent that it has universal appeal. Texans are the only "race of people" known to anthropologists who do not depend upon breeding for propagation. Like princes and lords, they can be made by "breath," plus a big white hat — which comparatively few Texans wear. A beef stew by a cook in San Antonio, Texas, may have a different flavor from that of a beef stew cooked in Pittsburgh, Pennsylvania, but the essential substances of potatoes and onions, with some suggestion of beef, are about the same, and geography has no effect on their digestibility.

A writer — a regional writer, if that term means anything — will whenever he matures exercise the critical faculty. I mean in the Matthew Arnold sense of appraisal rather than of praise, or, for that matter, of absolute condemnation. Understanding and sympathy are not eulogy. Mere glorification is on the same intellectual level as silver tongues and juke box music.

In using that word *intellectual,* one lays himself liable to the accusation of having forsaken democracy. For all that, "fundamental brainwork" is behind every respect-worthy piece of writing, whether it be a lightsome lyric that seems as careless as a redbird's flit or a formal epic, an impressionistic essay or a great novel that measures the depth of human destiny. Nonintellectual literature is as nonexistent as education without mental discipline, or as "character building" in a school that is slovenly in scholarship. Billboards along the highways of Texas advertise certain towns and cities as "cultural centers." Yet no chamber of commerce would consider advertising an intellectual center. The culture of a nineteenth-century finishing school for young ladies was divorced from intellect; genuine civilization is always informed by intellect. The American populace has been taught to believe that the more intellectual a professor is, the less common sense he has; nevertheless, if American democracy is preserved it will be preserved by thought and not by physics.

Editors of all but a few magazines of the country and publishers of most of the daily newspapers cry out for brightness and vitality and at the same time shut out critical ideas. They want intellect, but want it petrified. Happily, the publishers of books have not yet reached that form of delusion. In an article entitled "What Ideas Are Safe?" in the *Saturday Review of Literature* for November 5, 1949, Henry Steele Commager says:

If we establish a standard of safe thinking, we will end up with no thinking at all.... We cannot...have thought half slave and half free.... A nation which, in the name of loyalty or of patriotism or of any sincere and high-sounding ideal, discourages criticism and dissent, and puts a premium on acquiescence and conformity, is headed for disaster.

Unless a writer feels free, things will not come to him, he cannot burgeon on any subject whatsoever.

In 1834 Davy Crockett's *Autobiography* was published. It is one of the primary social documents of America. It is as much Davy Crockett, whether going ahead after bears in a Tennessee canebrake or going ahead after General Andrew Jackson in Congress, as the equally plain but also urbane *Autobiography* of Franklin is Benjamin Franklin. It is undiluted regionalism. It is provincial not only in subject but in point of view.

No provincial mind of this day could possibly write an autobiography or any other kind of book co-ordinate in value with Crockett's "classic in homespun." In his time, Crockett could exercise intelligence and still retain his provincial point of view. Provincialism was in the air over his land. In these changed times, something in the ambient air prevents any active intelligence from being unconscious of lands, peoples, struggles far beyond any province.

Not long after the Civil War, in Harris County, Texas, my father heard a bayou-billy yell out:

> Whoopee! Raised in a canebrake and suckled by a she-bear!
> The click of a six-shooter is music to my ear!
> The further up the creek you go, the worse they git,
> And I come from the head of it! Whoopee!

If it were now possible to find some section of country so far up above the forks of the creek that the owls mate there with the chickens, and if this section could send to Congress one of its provincials untainted by the outside world, he would, if at all intelligent, soon after arriving on Capitol Hill become aware of interdependencies between his remote province and the rest of the world.

Biographies of regional characters, stories turning on local customs, novels based on an isolated society, books of history and fiction going back to provincial simplicity will go on being written and published. But I do not believe it possible that a good one will henceforth come from a mind that does not in outlook transcend the region on which it is focused. That is not to imply that the processes of evolution have brought all parts of the world into such interrelationships that a writer cannot depict the manners and morals of a community up Owl Hoot Creek without enmeshing them with the complexities of the Atlantic Pact. Awareness of other times and other wheres, not insistence on that awareness, is the requisite. James M. Barrie said that he could not write a play until he got his people off on a kind of island, but had he not known about the mainland he could never have delighted us with the islanders — islanders, after all, for the night only. Patriotism of the right kind is still a fine thing; but, despite all gulfs, canyons, and curtains that separate nations, those nations and their provinces are all increasingly interrelated.

No sharp line of time or space, like that separating one century from another or the territory of one nation from that of another, can delimit the boundaries of any region to which any regionalist lays claim. Mastery, for instance, of certain locutions peculiar to the Southwest will take their user to the Aztecs, to Spain, and to the border of ballads and Sir Walter Scott's romances. I found that I could not comprehend the coyote as animal hero of Pueblo and Plains Indians apart from the Reynard of Aesop and Chaucer.

In a noble opinion respecting censorship and freedom of the press, handed down on March 18, 1949, Judge Curtis Bok of Pennsylvania said:

> It is no longer possible that free speech be guaranteed Federally and denied locally; under modern methods of instantaneous communication such a discrepancy makes no sense.... What is said in Pennsylvania may clarify an issue in California, and what is suppressed in California may leave us the worse in Pennsylvania. Unless a restriction on free speech be of national validity, it can no longer have any local validity whatever.

Among the qualities that any good regional writer has in common with other good writers of all places and times is intellectual integrity. Having it does not obligate him to speak out on all issues or, indeed, on any issue. He alone is to judge whether he will sport with Amaryllis in the shade or forsake her to write his own *Areopagitica*. Intellectual integrity expresses itself in the tune as well as argument, in choice of words — words honest and precise — as well as in ideas, in fidelity to human nature and the flowers of the fields as well as to principles, in facts reported more than in deductions proposed. Though a writer write on something as innocuous as the white snails that crawl up broomweed stalks and that roadrunners carry to certain rocks to crack and eat, his intellectual integrity, if he has it, will infuse the subject.

Nothing is too trivial for art, but good art treats nothing in a trivial way. Nothing is too provincial for the regional writer, but he cannot be provincial-minded toward it. Being provincial-minded may make him a typical provincial; it will prevent him from being a representative or skilful interpreter. Horace Greeley said that when the rules of the English language got in his way, they did not stand a chance.

We may be sure that if by violating the rules of syntax Horace Greeley sometimes added forcefulness to his editorials, he violated them deliberately and not in ignorance. Luminosity is not stumbled into. The richly savored and deliciously unlettered speech of Thomas Hardy's rustics was the creation of a master architect who had looked out over the ranges of fated mankind and looked also into hell. Thomas Hardy's ashes were placed in Westminster Abbey, but his heart, in accordance with a provision of his will, was buried in the churchyard of his own village.

I have never tried to define regionalism. Its blanket has been put over a great deal of worthless writing. Robert Frost has approached a satisfying conception. "The land is always in my bones," he said — the land of rock fences. But, "I am not a regionalist. I am a realmist. I write about realms of democracy and realms of the spirit." Those realms include The Woodpile, The Grindstone, Blueberries, Birches, and many other features of the land North of Boston.

To an extent, any writer anywhere must make his own world, no matter whether in fiction or nonfiction, prose or poetry. He must make something out of his subject. What he makes depends upon his creative power, integrated with a sense of form. The popular restriction of creative writing to fiction and verse is illogical. Carl Sandburg's life of Lincoln is immeasurably more creative in form and substance than his fanciful *Potato Face*. Intense exercise of his creative power sets, in a way, the writer apart from the life he is trying to sublimate. Becoming a Philistine will not enable a man to interpret Philistinism, though Philistines who own big presses think so. Sinclair Lewis knew Babbitt as Babbitt could never know either himself or Sinclair Lewis.

J. F. D.

The time of Mexican primroses
1952

1

A Declaration

IN THE UNIVERSITY of Texas I teach a course called "Life and Literature of the Southwest." About 1929 I had a brief guide to books concerning the Southwest mimeographed; in 1931 it was included by John William Rogers in a booklet entitled *Finding Literature on the Texas Plains*. After that I revised and extended the guide three or four times, during the process distributing several thousand copies of the mimeographed forms. Now the guide has grown too long, and I trust that this printing of it will prevent my making further additions — though within a short time new books will come out that should be added.

Yet the guide is fragmentary, incomplete, and in no sense a bibliography. Its emphases vary according to my own indifferences and ignorance as well as according to my own sympathies and knowledge. It is strong on the character and ways of life of the early settlers, on the growth of the soil, and on everything pertaining to the range; it is weak on information concerning politicians and on citations to studies which, in the manner of orthodox Ph.D. theses, merely transfer bones from one graveyard to another.

It is designed primarily to help people of the Southwest see significances in the features of the land to which they belong, to make their environments more interesting to them, their past more alive, to bring them to a realization of the values of their own cultural inheritance, and to stimulate them to observe. It includes most of the books about the Southwest that people in general would agree on as making good reading.

I have never had any idea of writing or teaching about my own section of the country merely as a patriotic duty. Without apologies, I would interpret it because I love it, because it interests me, talks to me, appeals to my imagination, warms my emotions; also because it seems to me that other people living in the Southwest will lead fuller and richer lives if they become aware of what it holds. I once thought that, so far as reading goes, I could live forever on the supernal beauty of Shelley's "The Cloud" and his soaring lines "To a Skylark," on the rich melancholy of Keats's "Ode to a Nightingale," on Cyrano de Bergerac's ideal of a free man, on Wordsworth's philosophy of nature — a philosophy that has illuminated for me the mesquite flats and oak-studded hills of Texas — on the adventures in Robert Louis Stevenson, the flavor and wit of Lamb's essays, the eloquent wisdom of Hazlitt, the dark mysteries of Conrad, the gaieties of Barrie, the melody of Sir Thomas Browne, the urbanity of Addison, the dash in Kipling, the mobility, the mightiness, the lightness, the humor, the humanity, the everything of Shakespeare, and a world of other delicious, high, beautiful, and inspiring things that English literature has bestowed upon us. That literature is still the richest of heritages; but literature is not enough.

Here I am living on a soil that my people have been living and working and dying on for more than a hundred years — the soil, as it happens, of Texas. My roots go down into this soil as deep as mesquite roots go. This soil has nourished me as the banks of the lovely Guadalupe River nourish cypress trees, as the Brazos bottoms nourish the wild peach, as the gentle slopes of East Texas nourish the sweet-smelling pines, as the barren, rocky ridges along the Pecos nourish the daggered lechuguilla. I am at home here, and I want not only to know about my home land, I want to live intelligently on it. I want certain data that will enable me to accommodate myself to it. Knowledge helps sympathy to achieve harmony. I am made more resolute by Arthur Hugh Clough's picture of the dripping sailor on the reeling mast, "On stormy nights when wild northwesters rave," but the winds that have bit into me have been dry Texas northers; and fantastic yarns about them, along with a cowboy's story of a herd of Longhorns drifting to death in front of one of them, come home to me and illuminate those northers like forked lightning playing along the top of black clouds in the night.

No informed person would hold that the Southwest can claim any considerable body of *pure literature* as its own. At the same time, the region has a distinct cultural inheritance, full of life and drama, told variously in books so numerous that their very existence would surprise many people who depend on the Book-of-the-Month Club for literary guidance. Any people have a right to their own cultural inheritance, though sheeplike makers of textbooks and sheeplike pedagogues of American literature have until recently, either wilfully or ignorantly, denied that right to the Southwest. Tens of thousands of students of the Southwest have been assigned endless pages on and listened to dronings over Cotton Mather, Increase Mather, Jonathan Edwards, Anne Bradstreet, and other dreary creatures of colonial New England who are utterly foreign to the genius of the Southwest. If nothing in written form pertaining to the Southwest existed at all, it would be more profitable for an inhabitant to go out and listen to coyotes singing at night in the prickly pear than to tolerate the Increase Mather kind of thing. It is very profitable to listen to coyotes anyhow. I rebelled years ago at having the tradition, the spirit, the meaning of the soil to which I belong utterly disregarded by interpreters of literature and at the same time having the Increase Mather kind of stuff taught as if it were important to our part of America. Happily the disregard is disappearing, and so is Increase Mather.

If they had to be rigorously classified into hard and fast categories, comparatively few of the books in the lists that follow would be rated as pure literature. Fewer would be rated as history. A majority of them are the stuff of history.

The stuff out of which history is made is generally more vital than formalized history, especially the histories habitually forced on students in public schools, colleges, and universities. There is no essential opposition between history and literature. The attempt to study a people's literature apart from their social and, to a less extent, their political history is as illogical as the lady who said she had read Romeo but had not yet got to Juliet. Nearly any kind of history is more important than formal literary history showing how in a literary way Abraham begat Isaac and Isaac begat Jacob. Any man of any time who has ever written with vigor has been immeasurably nearer to the dunghill on which he sank his talons while crowing than to all literary ancestors.

A great deal of chronicle writing that makes no pretense at being belles-lettres is really superior literature to much that is so classified. I will vote three times a day and all night for John C. Duval's *Adventures of Bigfoot Wallace*, Charlie Siringo's *Riata and Spurs*, James B. Gillett's *Six Years with the Texas Rangers*, and dozens of other straightaway chronicles of the Southwest in preference to "The Culprit Fay" and much other watery "literature" with which anthologies representing the earlier stages of American writing are padded. Ike Fridge's pamphlet story of his ridings for John Chisum— chief provider of cattle for Billy the Kid to steal — has more of the juice of reality in it and, therefore, more of literary virtue than some of James Fenimore Cooper's novels, and than some of James Russell Lowell's odes.

The one thing essential to writing if it is to be read, to art if it is to be looked at, is vitality. No critic or professor can be hired to pump vitality into any kind of human expression, but professors and critics have taken it out of many a human being who in his attempts to say something decided to be correct at the expense of being himself — being natural, being alive. The priests of literary conformity never had a chance at the homemade chronicles of the Southwest.

The orderly way in which to study the Southwest would be to take up first the land, its flora, fauna, climate, soils, rivers, etc., then the aborigines, next the exploring and settling Spaniards, and finally, after a hasty glance at the French, the English-speaking people who brought the Southwest to what it is today. We cannot proceed in this way, however. Neither the prairies nor the Indians who first hunted deer on them have left any records, other than hieroglyphic, as to their lives. Some late-coming men have written about them. Droughts and rains have had far more influence on all forms of life in the Southwest and on all forms of its development culturally and otherwise than all of the Coronado expeditions put together. I have emphasized the literature that reveals nature. My method has been to take up types and subjects rather than to follow chronology.

Chronology is often an impediment to the acquiring of useful knowledge. I am not nearly so much interested in what happened in Abilene, Kansas, in 1867 — the year that the first herds of Texas Longhorns over the Chisholm Trail found a market at that place — as I am in picking out of Abilene in 1867 some thing that reveals the character of the men who went up the trail, some thing that will illuminate certain phenomena along the trail human beings of the Southwest are going up today, some thing to awaken observation and to enrich with added meaning this corner of the earth of which we are the temporary inheritors.

By "literature of the Southwest" I mean writings that interpret the region, whether they have been produced by the Southwest or not. Many of them have not. What we are interested in is life in the Southwest, and any interpreter of that life, foreign or domestic, ancient or modern, is of value.

The term Southwest is variable because the boundaries of the Southwest are themselves fluid, expanding and contracting according to the point of view from which the Southwest is viewed and according to whatever common denominator is taken for defining it. The Spanish Southwest includes California, but California regards itself as more closely akin to the Pacific Northwest than to Texas; California is Southwest more in an antiquarian way than otherwise. From the point of view of the most picturesque and imagination-influencing occupation of the Southwest, the occupation of ranching, the Southwest might be said to run up into Montana. Certainly one will have to go up the trail to Montana to finish out the story of the Texas cowboy. Early in the nineteenth century the Southwest meant Tennessee, Georgia, and other frontier territory now regarded as strictly South. The men and women who "redeemed Texas from the wilderness" came principally from that region. The code of conduct they gave Texas was largely the code of the booming West. Considering the character of the Anglo-American people who took over the Southwest, the region is closer to Missouri than to Kansas, which is not Southwest in any sense but which has had a strong influence on Oklahoma. Chihuahua is more southwestern than large parts of Oklahoma. In *Our Southwest*, Erna Fergusson has a whole chapter on "What is the Southwest?" She finds Fort Worth to be in the Southwest but Dallas, thirty miles east, to be facing north and east. The principal areas of the Southwest are, to have done with air-minded reservations, Arizona, New Mexico, most of Texas, some of Oklahoma, and anything else north, south, east, or west that anybody wants to bring in. The boundaries of cultures and rainfall never follow survey lines. In talking about the Southwest I naturally incline to emphasize the Texas part of it.

Life is fluid, and definitions that would apprehend it must also be. Yet I will venture one definition — not the only one — of an educated person. An educated person is one who can view with interest and intelligence the phenomena of life about him. Like people elsewhere, the people of the Southwest find the features of the land on which they live blank or full of pictures according to the amount of interest and intelligence with which they view the features. Intelligence cannot be acquired, but interest can; and data for interest and intelligence to act upon are entirely acquirable.

"Studies perfect nature," Bacon said. "Nature follows

art" to the extent that most of us see principally what our attention has been called to. I might never have noticed rose-purple snow between shadows if I had not seen a picture of that kind of snow. I had thought white the only natural color of snow. I cannot think of yew trees, which I have never seen, without thinking of Wordsworth's poem on three yew trees.

Nobody has written a memorable poem on the mesquite. Yet the mesquite has entered into the social, economic, and aesthetic life of the land; it has made history and has been painted by artists. In the homely chronicles of the Southwest its thorns stick, its roots burn into bright coals, its trunks make fence posts, its lovely leaves wave. To live beside this beautiful, often pernicious, always interesting and highly characteristic tree — or bush — and to know nothing of its significance is to be cheated out of a part of life. It is but one of a thousand factors peculiar to the Southwest and to the land's cultural inheritance.

For a long time, as he tells in his *Narrative*, Cabeza de Vaca was a kind of prisoner to coastal Indians of Texas. Annually, during the season when prickly pear apples (*tunas*, or Indian figs, as they are called in books) were ripe, these Indians would go upland to feed on the fruit. During his sojourn with them Cabeza de Vaca went along. He describes how the Indians would dig a hole in the ground, squeeze the fruit out of *tunas* into the hole, and then swill up big drinks of it. Long ago the Indians vanished, but prickly pears still flourish over millions of acres of land. The prickly pear is one of the characteristic growths of the Southwest. Strangers look at it and regard it as odd. Painters look at it in bloom or in fruit and strive to capture the colors. During the droughts ranchmen singe the thorns off its leaves, using a flame-throwing machine, easily portable by a man on foot, fed from a small gasoline tank. From Central Texas on down into Central America prickly pear acts as host for the infinitesimal insect called cochineal, which supplied the famous dyes of Aztec civilization.

A long essay might be written on prickly pear. It weaves in and out of many chronicles of the Southwest. A. J. Sowell, one of the best chroniclers of Texas pioneer life, tells in his life of Bigfoot Wallace how that picturesque ranger captain once took one of his wounded men away from an army surgeon because the surgeon would not apply prickly pear poultices to the wound. In *Rangers and Pioneers of Texas,* Sowell narrates how rattlesnakes were so large and numerous in a great prickly pear flat out from the Nueces River that rangers pursuing bandits had to turn back. Nobody has written a better description of a prickly pear flat than O. Henry in his story of "The Caballero's Way."

People may look at prickly pear, and it will be just prickly pear and nothing more. Or they may look at it and find it full of significances; the mere sight of a prickly pear may call up a chain of incidents, facts, associations. A mind that can thus look out on the common phenomena of life is rich, and all of the years of the person whose mind is thus stored will be more interesting and full.

Cabeza de Vaca's *Narrative,* the chronicles of A. J. Sowell, and O. Henry's story are just three samples of southwestern literature that bring in prickly pear. No active-minded person who reads any one of these three samples will ever again look at prickly pear in the same light that he looked at it before he read. Yet prickly pear is just one of hundreds of manifestations of life in the Southwest that writers have commented on, told stories about, dignified with significance.

Cotton no longer has the economic importance to Texas that it once had. Still, it is mighty important. In the minds of millions of farm people of the South, cotton and the boll weevil are associated. The boll weevil was once a curse; then it came to be somewhat regarded as a disguised blessing — in limiting production.

> De first time I seen de boll weevil,
>   He was a-settin' on de square.
> Next time I seen him, he had all his family dere —
>   Jest a-lookin' foh a home, jest a-lookin' foh a home.

A man dependent on cotton for a living and having that living threatened by the boll weevil will not be much interested in ballads, but for the generality of people this boll weevil ballad — the entirety of which is a kind of life history of the insect — is, while delightful in itself, a veritable storybook on the weevil. Without the ballad, the weevil's effect on economic history would be unchanged; but as respects mind and imagination, the ballad gives the weevil all sorts of significances. The ballad is a part of the literature of the Southwest.

But I am assigning too many motives of self-improvement to reading. People read for fun, for pleasure. The literature of the Southwest affords bully reading.

"If I had read as much as other men, I would know as little," Thomas Hobbes is credited with having said. A student in the presence of Bishop E. D. Mouzon was telling about the scores and scores of books he had read. At a pause the bishop shook his long, wise head and remarked, "My son, when *do* you get time to think?" Two of the best educated men I have ever had the fortune of talking with were neither schooled nor widely read. They were extraordinary observers. One was a plainsman, Charles Goodnight; the other was a borderer, Don Alberto Guajardo, in part educated by an old Lipan Indian.

But here are the books. I list them not so much to give knowledge as to direct people with intellectual curiosity and with interest in their own land to the sources of knowledge; not to create life directly, but to point out where it has been created or copied. On some of the books I have made brief observations. Those observations can never be nearly so important to a reader as the development of his own powers of observation. With something of an apologetic feeling I confess that I have read, in my way, most of the books. I should probably have been a wiser and better informed man had I spent more time out with the grasshoppers, horned toads, and coyotes.

November 5, 1942   J. FRANK DOBIE

2

Interpreters of the Land

"HE'S FOR A JIG or a tale of bawdry, or he sleeps." Thought employs ideas, but having an idea is not the same thing as thinking. A rooster in a pen of hens has an idea. Thought has never been so popular with mankind as horse opera, horse play, the main idea behind sheep's eyes. Far be it from me to feel contempt for people who cannot and do not want to think. The human species has not yet evolved to the stage at which thought is natural. I am far more at ease lying in grass and gazing without thought process at clouds than in sitting in a chair trying to be logical. Just the same, free play of mind upon life is the essence of good writing, and intellectual activity is synonymous with critical interpretations.

To the constant disregard of thought, Americans of the mid-twentieth century have added positive opposition. Critical ideas are apt to make any critic suspected of being subversive. The Southwest, Texas especially, is more articulately aware of its land spaces than of any other feature pertaining to itself. Yet in the realm of government, the Southwest has not produced a single spacious thinker. So far as the cultural ancestry of the region goes, the South has been arid of thought since the time of Thomas Jefferson, the much talked-of mind of John C. Calhoun being principally casuistic; on another side, derivatives from the Spanish Inquisition could contribute to thought little more than tribal medicine men have contributed.

Among historians of the Southwest the general rule has been to be careful with facts and equally careful in avoiding thought-provoking interpretations. In the multitudinous studies on Spanish-American history all padres are "good" and all conquistadores are "intrepid," and that is about as far as interpretation goes. The one state book of the Southwest that does not chloroform ideas is Erna Fergusson's *New Mexico: A Pageant of Three Peoples* (Knopf, New York, 1952). Essayical in form, it treats only of the consequential. It evaluates from the point of view of good taste, good sense, and an urbane comprehension of democracy. The subject is provincial, but the historian transcends all provincialism. Her sympathy does not stifle conclusions unusable in church or chamber of commerce propaganda. In brief, a cultivated mind can take pleasure in this interpretation of New Mexico — and that marks it as a solitary among the histories of neighboring states.

The outstanding historical interpreter of the Southwest is Walter Prescott Webb, of the University of Texas. *The Great Plains* utilizes chronology to explain the presence of man on the plains; it is primarily a study in cause and effect, of water and drought, of adaptations and lack of adaptations, of the land's growth into human imagination as well as economic institutions. Webb uses facts to get at meanings. He fulfils Emerson's definition of Scholar: "Man Thinking." In *Divided We Stand* he goes into machinery, the feudalism of corporation-dominated economy, the economic supremacy of the North over the South and the West. In *The Great Frontier* (Houghton Mifflin, Boston, 1952) he considers the Western Hemisphere as a frontier for Europe — a frontier that brought about the rise of democracy and capitalism and that, now vanished as a frontier, foreshadows the vanishment of democracy and capitalism.

In *Virgin Land: The American West as Symbol and Myth* (Harvard University Press, Cambridge, Massachusetts, 1950) Henry Nash Smith plows deep. But the tools of this humanistic historian are of delicate finish rather than of horsepower. To him, thinking is a joyful process and lucidity out of complexity is natural. He compasses Parrington's *Main Currents in American Thought* and Beadle's Dime

Novels along with agriculture and manufacturing. Excepting the powerful books by Walter Prescott Webb, not since Frederick Jackson Turner, in 1893, presented his famous thesis on "The Significance of the Frontier in American History" has such a revealing evaluation of frontier movements appeared. As a matter of fact, Henry Nash Smith leaves Turner's ideas on the dependence of democracy upon farmers without more than one leg to stand upon. Not being a King Canute, he does not take sides for or against social evolution. With the clearest eyes imaginable, he looks into it. Turner's *The Frontier in American History* (1920) has been a fertile begetter of interpretations of history.

Instead of being the usual kind of jokesmith book or concatenation of tall tales, *Folk Laughter on the American Frontier* by Mody C. Boatright (Macmillan, New York, 1949) goes into the human and social significances of humor. Of boastings, anecdotal exaggerations, hide-and-hair metaphors, stump and pulpit parables, tenderfoot baitings, and the like there is plenty, but thought plays upon them and arranges them into patterns of social history.

Mary Austin (1868-1934) is an interpreter of nature, which for her includes naturally placed human beings as much as naturally placed antelopes and cacti. She wrote *The American Rhythm* on the theory that authentic poetry expresses the rhythms of that patch of earth to which the poet is rooted. Rhythm is experience passed into the subconscious and is "distinct from our intellectual perception of it." Before they can make true poetry, English-speaking Americans will be in accord with "the run of wind in tall grass" as were the Pueblo Indians when Europeans discovered them. But Mary Austin's primary importance is not as a theorist. Her spiritual depth is greater than her intellectual. She is a translator of nature through concrete observations. She interprets through character sketches, folk tales, novels. "Anybody can write facts about a country," she said. She infuses fact with understanding and imagination. In *Lost Borders, The Land of Little Rain, The Land of Journey's Ending,* and

The Flock the land itself often seems to speak, but often she gets in its way. She sees "with an eye made quiet by the power of harmony." *Earth Horizons,* a stubborn book, is Mary Austin's inner autobiography. *The Beloved House,* by T. M. Pearce (Caxton, Caldwell, Idaho, 1940), is an understanding biography.

Joseph Wood Krutch of Columbia University spent a year in Arizona, near Tucson. Instead of talking about his *The Desert Year* (Sloane, New York, 1952), I quote a representative paragraph:

In New England the struggle for existence is visibly the struggle of plant with plant, each battling his neighbor for sunlight and for the spot of ground which, so far as moisture and nourishment are concerned, would support them all. Here, the contest is not so much of plant against plant as of plant against inanimate nature. The limiting factor is not the neighbor but water; and I wonder if this is, perhaps, one of the things which makes this country seem to enjoy a kind of peace one does not find elsewhere. The struggle of living thing against living thing can be distressing in a way that a mere battle with the elements is not. If some great clump of cactus dies this summer it will be because the cactus has grown beyond the capacity of its roots to get water, not because one green fellow creature has bested it in some limb-to-limb struggle. In my more familiar East the crowding of the countryside seems almost to parallel the crowding of the cities. Out here there is, even in nature, no congestion.

Southwest, by Laura Adams Armer (New York, 1935, OP) came from long living and brooding in desert land. It says something beautiful.

Talking to the Moon, by John Joseph Mathews (University of Chicago Press, 1945) is set in the blackjack country of eastern Oklahoma. This Oxford scholar of Osage blood built his ranch house around a fireplace, flanked by shelves of books. His observations are of the outside, but they are informed by reflections made beside a fire. They are not bookish at all, but the spirits of great writers mingle with echoes of coyote wailing and wood-thrush singing.

Sky Determines: An Interpretation of the Southwest, by Ross Calvin (New York, 1934; republished by the University

of New Mexico Press) lives up to its striking title. The intro-
ductory words suggest the essence of the book:

In New Mexico whatever is both old and peculiar appears upon exami-
nation to have a connection with the arid climate. Peculiarities range
from the striking adaptations of the flora onward to those of fauna,
and on up to those the human animal. Sky determines. And the
writer once having picked up the trail followed it with certainty, and
indeed almost inevitably, as it led from ecology to anthropology and
economics.

Cultivated intellect is the highest form of civilization.
It is inseparable from the arts, literature, architecture. In any
civilized land, birds, trees, flowers, animals, places, human
contributors to life out of the past, all are richer and more
significant because of representations through literature and
art. No literate person can listen to a skylark over an English
meadow without hearing in its notes the melodies of Chaucer
and Shelley. As the Southwest advances in maturity of mind
and civilization, the features of the land take on accretions
from varied interpreters.

It is not necessary for an interpreter to write a whole
book about a feature to bring out its significance. We need
more gossipy books — something in the manner of *Piñon
Country* by Haniel Long (Duell, Sloan and Pearce, New
York, 1941), in which one can get a swift slant on Billy the
Kid, smell the piñon trees, feel the deeply religious attitude
toward his corn patch of a Zuñi Indian. Roy Bedichek's
chapters on the mockingbird, in *Adventures with a Texas
Naturalist*, are like rich talk under a tree on a pleasant patch
of ground staked out for his claim by an April-voiced mockingbird. In *The Voice of the Coyote* I tried to compass the
whole animal, and I should think that the "Father of Song-
Making" chapter might make coyote music and the night
more interesting and beautiful for any listener. Intelligent
writers often interpret without set purpose, and many books
under various categories in this *Guide* are interpretative.

3

General Helps

THERE IS no chart to the Life and Literature of the Southwest. An attempt to put it all into an alphabetically arranged encyclopedia would be futile. All guides to knowledge are too long or too short. This one at the outset adds to its length — perhaps to its usefulness — by citing other general reference works and a few anthologies.

Books of the Southwest: A General Bibliography, by Mary Tucker, published by J. J. Augustin, New York, 1937, is better on Indians and the Spanish period than on Anglo-American culture. *Southwest Heritage: A Literary History with Bibliography,* by Mabel Major, Rebecca W. Smith, and T. M. Pearce, University of New Mexico Press, Albuquerque, 1938, revised 1948, takes up the written material under the time-established heads of Fiction, Poetry, Drama, etc., with due respect to chronological development. *A Treasury of Southern Folklore,* 1949, and *A Treasury of Western Folklore,* 1951, both edited by B. A. Botkin and both published by Crown, New York, are so liberal in the extensions of folklore and so voluminous that they amount to literary anthologies.

Of possible use in working out certain phases of life and literature common to the Southwest as well as to the West and Middle West are the following academic treatises: *The Frontier in American Literature,* by Lucy Lockwood Hazard, New York, 1927; *The Literature of the Middle Western Frontier,* by Ralph Leslie Rusk, New York, 1925; *The Prairie and the Making of Middle America,* by Dorothy Anne Dondore, Cedar Rapids, Iowa, 1926; *The Literature of the Rocky*

Mountain West 1803-1903, by L. J. Davidson and P. Bostwick, Caldwell, Idaho, 1939; and *The Rediscovery of the Frontier*, by Percy H. Boynton, Chicago, 1931. Anyone interested in vitality in any phase of American writing will find Vernon L. Parrington's *Main Currents in American Thought* (three vols.), New York, 1927-39, an opener-up of avenues.

Perhaps the best anthology of southwestern narratives is *Golden Tales of the Southwest*, selected by Mary L. Becker, New York, 1939. Two anthologies of southwestern writings are *Southwesterners Write*, edited by T. M. Pearce and A. P. Thomason, University of New Mexico Press, Albuquerque, 1946, and *Roundup Time*, edited by George Sessions Perry, Whittlesey House, New York, 1943. Themes common to the Southwest are represented in *Western Prose and Poetry*, an anthology put together by Rufus A. Coleman, New York, 1932, and in *Mid Country: Writings from the Heart of America*, edited by Lowry C. Wimberly, University of Nebraska Press, Lincoln, 1945.

For the southern tradition that has flowed into the Southwest Franklin J. Meine's *Tall Tales of the Southwest*, New York, 1930, OP, is the best anthology published. It is the best anthology of any kind that I know of. *A Southern Treasury of Life and Literature*, selected by Stark Young, New York, 1937, brings in Texas.

Anthologies of poetry are listed under the heading of "Poetry and Drama." The outstanding state bibliography of the region is *A Bibliography of Texas*, by C. W. Raines, Austin, 1896. Since this is half a century behind the times, its usefulness is limited. At that, it is more useful than the shiftless, hit-and-miss, ignorance-revealing *South of Forty: From the Mississippi to the Rio Grande: A Bibliography*, by Jesse L. Rader, Norman, Oklahoma, 1947. Henry R. Wagner's *The Plains and the Rockies*, "a contribution to the bibliography of original narratives of travel and adventure, 1800-1865," which came out 1920-21, was revised and extended by Charles L. Camp and reprinted in 1937. It is stronger on overland travel than on anything else, only in part covers the

Southwest, and excludes a greater length of time than Raines's *Bibliography*. Now published by Long's College Book Co., Columbus, Ohio.

Mary G. Boyer's *Arizona in Literature*, Glendale, California, 1934, is an anthology that runs toward six hundred pages. *Texas Prose Writings*, by Sister M. Agatha, Dallas, 1936, OP, is a meaty, critical survey. L. W. Payne's handbook-sized *A Survey of Texas Literature*, Chicago, 1928, is complemented by a chapter entitled "Literature and Art in Texas" by J. Frank Dobie in *The Book of Texas*, New York, 1929. OP.

A Guide to Materials Bearing on Cultural Relations in New Mexico, University of New Mexico Press, Albuquerque, 1944, is so logical and liberal-minded that in some respects it amounts to a bibliography of the whole Southwest; it recognizes the overriding of political boundaries by ideas, human types, and other forms of culture. The *New Mexico Quarterly*, published by the University of New Mexico, furnishes periodically a bibliographical record of contemporary literature of the Southwest. *New Mexico's Own Chronicle*, edited by Maurice G. Fulton and Paul Horgan (Dallas, 1937, OP), is an anthology strong on the historical side.

In the lists that follow, the symbol OP indicates that the book is out of print. Many old books obviously out of print are not so tagged.

4

Indian Culture; Pueblos and Navajos

THE LITERATURE on the subject of Indians is so extensive and ubiquitous that, unless a student of Americana is pursuing it, he may find it more troublesome to avoid than to get hold of. The average old-timer has for generations regarded Indian scares and fights as the most important theme for reminiscences. County-minded historians have taken the same point of view. The Bureau of American Ethnology of the Smithsonian Institution has buried records of Indian beliefs, ceremonies, mythology, and other folklore in hundreds of tomes; laborious, literal-minded scholars of other institutions have been as assiduous. In all this lore and tabulation of facts, the Indian folk themselves have generally been dried out.

The Anglo-American's policy toward the Indian was to kill him and take his land, perhaps make a razor-strop out of his hide. The Spaniard's policy was to baptize him, take his land, enslave him, and appropriate his women. Any English-speaking frontiersman who took up with the Indians was dubbed "squaw man"—a term of sinister connotations. Despite pride in descending from Pocahontas and in the vaunted Indian blood of such individuals as Will Rogers, crossbreeding between Anglo-Americans and Indians has been restricted, as compared, for instance, with the interdicted crosses between white men and black women. The Spaniards, on the other hand, crossed in battalions with the Indians, generating *mestizo* (mixed-blooded) nations, of which Mexico is the chief example.

As a result, the English-speaking occupiers of the land have in general absorbed directly only a minimum of Indian culture—nothing at all comparable to the Uncle Remus stories and characters and the spiritual songs and the blues music from the Negroes. Grandpa still tells how his own grandpa saved or lost his scalp during a Comanche horse-stealing raid in the light of the moon; Boy Scouts hunt for Indian arrowheads; every section of the country has a bluff called Lovers' Leap, where, according to legend, a pair of forlorn Indian lovers, or perhaps only one of the pair, dived to death; the maps all show Caddo Lake, Kiowa Peak, Squaw Creek, Tehuacana Hills, Nacogdoches town, Cherokee County, Indian Gap, and many another place name derived from Indian days. All such contacts with Indian life are exterior. Three forms of Indian culture are, however, weaving into the life patterns of America.

(1) The Mexicans have naturally inherited and assimilated Indian lore about plants, animals, places, all kinds of human relationships with the land. Through the Mexican medium, with which he is becoming more sympathetic, the gringo is getting the ages-old Indian culture.

(2) The Pueblo and Navajo Indians in particular are impressing their arts, crafts, and ways of life upon special groups of Americans living near them, and these special groups are transmitting some of their acquisitions. The special groups incline to be arty and worshipful, but they express a salutary revolt against machined existence and they have done much to revive dignity in Indian life. Offsetting dilettantism, the Museum of New Mexico and associated institutions and artists and other individuals have fostered Indian pottery, weaving, silversmithing, dancing, painting, and other arts and crafts. Superior craftsmanship can now depend upon a fairly reliable market; the taste of American buyers has been somewhat elevated.

> O mountains, pure and holy, give me
> a song, a strong and holy song to bless
> my flock and bring the rain!

This is from "Navajo Holy Song," as rendered by Edith

Hart Mason. It expresses a spiritual content in Indian life far removed from the We and God, Incorporated form of religion ordained by the National Association of Manufacturers.

(3) The wild freedom, mobility, and fierce love of liberty of the mounted Indians of the Plains will perhaps always stir imaginations—something like the charging Cossacks, the camping Arabs, and the migrating Tartars. There is no romance in Indian fights east of the Mississippi. The mounted Plains Indians always made a big hit in Buffalo Bill's Wild West Show. Little boys still climb into their seats and cry out when red horsemen of the Plains ride across the screen.

See "Apaches, Comanches, and Other Plains Indians," "Mountain Men."

APPLEGATE, FRANK G. *Indian Stories from the Pueblos,* Philadelphia, 1929. Charming. OP.

ASTROV, MARGOT (editor), *The Winged Serpent,* John Day, New York, 1946. An anthology of prose and poetry by American Indians. Here are singular expressions of beauty and dignity.

AUSTIN, MARY. *The Trail Book,* 1918, OP; *One-Smoke Stories,* 1934, Houghton Mifflin, Boston. Delightful folk tales, each leading to a vista.

BANDELIER, A. F. *The Delight Makers,* 1918, Dodd, Mead, New York. Historical fiction on ancient pueblo life.

COOLIDGE, DANE and MARY. *The Navajo Indians,* Boston, 1930. Readable; bibliography. OP.

COOLIDGE, MARY ROBERTS. *The Rain-Makers,* Boston, 1929. OP. This thorough treatment of the Indians of Arizona and New Mexico contains an excellent account of the Hopi snake ceremony for bringing rain. During any severe drought numbers of Christians in the Southwest pray without snakes. It always rains eventually — and the prayer-makers naturally take the credit. The Hopis put on a more spectacular show. See Dr. Walter Hough's *The Hopi Indians,* Cedar Rapids, Iowa, 1915. OP.

CUSHING, FRANK HAMILTON. *Zuñi Folk Tales,* 1901; reprinted, 1931, by Knopf, New York. *My Adventures in Zuñi,* Santa Fe, 1941. *Zuñi Breadstuff,* Museum of the American Indian, New York, 1920. Cushing had rare imagination and sympathy. His retellings of tales are far superior to verbatim recordings. *Zuñi Breadstuff* reveals more of Indian spirituality than any other book I can name. All OP.

DeHUFF, ELIZABETH. *Tay Tay's Tales,* 1922; *Tay Tay's Memories,* 1924. OP.

DOUGLAS, FREDERIC H., and d'HARNONCOURT, RENÉ. *Indian Art of the United States,* Simon and Schuster, New York, 1941.

DYK, WALTER. *Son of Old Man Hat,* New York, 1938. OP.

FERGUSSON, ERNA. *Dancing Gods,* Knopf, New York, 1931. Erna Fergusson is always illuminating.

FOREMAN, GRANT. *Indians and Pioneers,* 1930, and *Advancing the Frontier,* University of Oklahoma Press, Norman, 1933. Grant Foreman is prime authority on the so-called "Civilized Tribes." University of Oklahoma Press has published a number of excellent volumes in "The Civilization of the American Indian" series.

GILLMOR, FRANCES, and WETHERILL, LOUISA WADE. *Traders to the Navajos,* Boston, 1936; reprinted by University of New Mexico Press, Albuquerque, 1952. An account not only of the trading post Wetherills but of the Navajos as human beings, with emphasis on their spiritual qualities.

GODDARD, P. E. *Indians of the Southwest,* New York, 1921. Excellent outline of exterior facts. OP.

HAMILTON, CHARLES (editor). *Cry of the Thunderbird,* Macmillan, New York, 1951. An anthology of writings by Indians containing many interesting leads.

HEWETT, EDGAR L. *Ancient Life in the American Southwest,* Indianapolis, 1930. OP. A master work in both archeology and Indian nature. (With Bertha P. Dretton) *The Pueblo Indian World,* University of New Mexico Press, Albuquerque, 1945.

HODGE, F. W. *Handbook of American Indians North of Mexico*, Washington, D. C., 1907. Indispensable encyclopedia, by a very great scholar and a very fine gentleman. OP.

LaBARRE, WESTON. *The Peyote Cult*, Yale University Press, New Haven, 1938.

LaFARGE, OLIVER. *Laughing Boy*, Boston, 1929. The Navajo in fiction.

LUMMIS, C. F. *Mesa, Cañon, and Pueblo*, New York, 1925; *Pueblo Indian Folk Tales*, New York, 1910. Lummis, though self-vaunting and opinionated, opens windows.

MATTHEWS, WASHINGTON. *Navajo Legends*, Boston, 1897; *Navajo Myths, Prayers and Songs*, Berkeley, California, 1907.

MOONEY, JAMES. *Myths of the Cherokees*, in Nineteenth Annual Report of the Bureau of Ethnology, Washington, 1902. Outstanding writing.

NELSON, JOHN LOUW. *Rhythm for Rain*, Boston, 1937. Based on ten years spent with the Hopi Indians, this study of their life is a moving story of humanity. OP.

PEARCE, J. E. *Tales That Dead Men Tell*, University of Texas Press, Austin, 1935. Eloquent, liberating to the human mind; something rare for Texas scholarship. Pearce was professor of anthropology at the University of Texas, an emancipator from prejudices and ignorance. It is a pity that all the college students who are forced by the bureaucrats of Education — Education spelled with a capital E — "the unctuous elaboration of the obvious" — do not take anthropology instead. Collegians would then stand a chance of becoming educated.

PETRULLO, VICENZO. *The Diabolic Root: A Study of Peyotism, the New Indian Religion, among the Delawares*, University of Pennsylvania Press, Philadelphia, 1934. The use of peyote has now spread northwest into Canada. See Milly Peacock Stenberg's *The Peyote Culture among Wyoming Indians*, University of Wyoming Publications, Laramie, 1946, for bibliography.

REICHARD, GLADYS A. *Spider Woman,* 1934, and *Dezba, Woman of the Desert,* 1939. Both honest, both OP.

SIMMONS, LEO W. (editor). *Sun Chief: The Autobiography of a Hopi Indian,* Yale University Press, New Haven, 1942. The clearest view into the mind and living ways, including sex life, of an Indian that has been published. Few autobiographers have been clearer; not one has been franker. A singular human document.

5

Apaches, Comanches, and Other Plains Indians

THE APACHES and the bareback Indians of the Plains were extraordinary *hombres del campo*—men of the outdoors, plainsmen, woodsmen, trailers, hunters, endurers. They knew some phases of nature with an intimacy that few civilized naturalists ever attain to. It is unfortunate that most of the literature about them is from their enemies. Yet an enemy often teaches a man more than his friends and makes him work harder.

See "Indian Culture," "Texas Rangers."

BOURKE, JOHN G. *On the Border with Crook,* London, 1892. Reprinted by Long's College Book Co., Columbus, Ohio. A truly great book, on both Apaches and Arizona frontier. Bourke had amplitude, and he knew.

BUCKELEW, F. M. *The Indian Captive,* Bandera, Texas, 1925. Homely and realistic. OP.

CATLIN, GEORGE. *Letters and Notes on the Manners, Customs and Conditions of the North American Indians, Written during Eight Years' Travel, 1832-39,* 1841. Despite many strictures, Catlin's two volumes remain standard. I am pleased to find Frank Roe, in *The North American Buffalo,* standing up for him. In *Pursuit of the Horizon: A Life of George Catlin, Painter and Recorder of the American Indian,* New York, 1948, Loyd Haberly fails in evaluating evidence but brings out the man's career and character.

CLUM, WOODWORTH. *Apache Agent,* Boston, 1936. Worthy autobiography of a noble understander of the Apache people. OP.

COMFORT, WILL LEVINGTON. *Apache*, Dutton, New York, 1931. Noble; vivid; semifiction.

DAVIS, BRITTON. *The Truth about Geronimo*, Yale University Press, New Haven, 1929. Davis helped run Geronimo down.

DESHIELDS, JAMES T. *Cynthia Ann Parker*, St. Louis, 1886; reprinted 1934. Good narrative of noted woman captive. OP.

DOBIE, J. FRANK. *The Mustangs*, Little, Brown, Boston, 1952. The opening chapters of this book distil a great deal of research by scholars on Plains Indian acquisition of horses, riding, and raiding.

GRINNELL, GEORGE BIRD. *The Cheyenne Indians*, New Haven, 1923. This two-volume work supersedes *The Fighting Cheyennes*, 1915. It is noble, ample, among the most select books on Plains Indians. *Blackfoot Lodge Tales: The Story of a Prairie People*, 1892, shows Grinnell's skill as storyteller at its best. *Pawnee Hero Stories and Folk Tales*, 1893, is hardly an equal but it reveals the high values of life held by representatives of the original plainsmen. *The Story of the Indian*, 1895, is a general survey. All OP. Grinnell's knowledge and power as a writer on Indians and animals has not been sufficiently recognized. He combined in a rare manner scholarship, plainsmanship, and the worldliness of publishing.

George Catlin, in *North American Indians* (1841)

HALEY, J. EVETTS. *Fort Concho and the Texas Frontier,* San Angelo Standard-Times, San Angelo, Texas, 1952. Mainly a history of military activities against Comanches and other tribes, laced with homilies on the free enterprise virtues of the conquerors.

LEE, NELSON. *Three Years among the Comanches,* 1859.

LEHMAN, HERMAN. *Nine Years with the Indians,* Bandera, Texas, 1927. Best captive narrative of the Southwest.

LOCKWOOD, FRANK C. *The Apache Indians,* Macmillan, New York, 1938. Factual history.

LONG LANCE, CHIEF BUFFALO CHILD. *Long Lance,* New York, 1928. OP. Long Lance was a Blackfoot only by adoption, but his imagination incorporated him into tribal life more powerfully than blood could have. He is said to have been a North Carolina mixture of Negro and Croatan Indian; he was a magnificent specimen of manhood with swart Indian complexion. He fought in the Canadian army during World War I and thus became acquainted with the Blackfeet. No matter what the facts of his life, he wrote a vivid and moving autobiography of a Blackfoot Indian in whom the spirit of the tribe and the natural life of the Plains during buffalo days were incorporated. In 1932 in the California home of Anita Baldwin, daughter of the spectacular "Lucky" Baldwin, he absented himself from this harsh world by a pistol shot.

LOWIE, ROBERT H. *The Crow Indians,* New York, 1935. This scholar and anthropologist lived with the Crow Indians to obtain intimate knowledge and then wrote this authoritative book. OP.

McALLISTER, J. GILBERT. "Kiowa-Apache Tales," in *The Sky Is My Tipi,* edited by Mody C. Boatright (Texas Folklore Society Publication XXII), Southern Methodist University Press, Dallas, 1949. Wise in exposition; true-to-humanity and delightful in narrative.

McGILLICUDDY, JULIA B. *McGillicuddy Agent,* Stanford University Press, California, 1941. Dr. Valentine T. McGillicuddy, Scotch in stubbornness, honesty, efficiency, and individualism, was U.S. Indian agent to the Sioux and knew them to the bottom. In the end he was defeated by the army mind and the bloodsuckers known as the "Indian Ring." The elements of nobility that distinguish the man distinguish his wife's biography of him.

McLAUGHLIN, JAMES. *My Friend the Indian*, 1910, 1926. OP. McLaughlin was U.S. Indian agent and inspector for half a century. Despite priggishness, he had genuine sympathy for the Indians; he knew the Sioux, Nez Percés, and Cheyennes intimately, and few books on Indian plainsmen reveal so much as his.

MARRIOTT, ALICE. *The Ten Grandmothers*, University of Oklahoma Press, Norman, 1945. Narratives of the Kiowas— a complement to James Mooney's *Calendar History of the Kiowa Indians*, in Seventeenth Annual Report of the Bureau of Ethnology, Washington, 1893. Alice Marriott, author of other books on Indians, combines ethnological science with the art of writing.

MATHEWS, JOHN JOSEPH. *Wah'Kon-Tah: The Osage and the White Man's Road*, University of Oklahoma Press, 1932. This book of essays on the character of and certain noble characters among the Great Osages, including their upright agent Leban J. Miles, has profound spiritual qualities.

NEIHARDT, JOHN G. *Black Elk Speaks*, New York, 1932. OP. Black Elk was a holy man of the Ogalala Sioux. The story of his life as he told it to understanding John G. Neihardt is more of mysteries and spiritual matters than of mundane affairs.

RICHARDSON, R. N. *The Comanche Barrier to the South Plains*, Glendale, California, 1933. Factual history.

RISTER, CARL C. *Border Captives*, University of Oklahoma Press, Norman, 1940.

RUXTON, GEORGE F. *Adventures in Mexico and the Rocky Mountains*, London, 1847. Vivid on Comanche raids. See Ruxton in "Surge of Life in the West."

SCHULTZ, J. W. *My Life as an Indian*, 1907. OP. In this autobiographical narrative of the life of a white man with a

Blackfoot woman, facts have probably been arranged, incidents added. Whatever his method, the author achieved a remarkable human document. It is true not only to Indian life in general but in particular to the life of a "squaw man" and his loved and loving mate. Among other authentic books by Schultz is *With the Indians of the Rockies,* Houghton Mifflin, Boston, 1912.

SMITH, C. L. and J. D. *The Boy Captives,* Bandera, Texas, 1927. A kind of classic in homeliness. OP.

VESTAL, STANLEY. *Sitting Bull,* Houghton Mifflin, Boston, 1932. Excellent biography. OP.

WALLACE, ERNEST, and HOEBEL, E. ADAMSON. *The Comanches: Lords of the South Plains,* University of Oklahoma Press, Norman, 1952. A wide-compassing and interesting book on a powerful and interesting people.

WELLMAN, PAUL I. *Death on the Prairie* (1934), *Death in the Desert* (1935); both reprinted in *Death on Horseback,* 1947. All OP. Graphic history, mostly in narrative, of the struggle of Plains and Apache Indians to hold their homelands against the whites.

WILBARGER, J. W. *Indian Depredations in Texas,* 1889; reprinted by Steck, Austin, 1936. Its stirring narratives made this a household book among Texans of the late nineteenth century.

6

Spanish-Mexican Strains

THE MEXICAN Revolution that began in 1910 resulted in a rich development of the native cultural elements of Mexico, the art of Diego Rivera being one of the highlights of this development. The native culture is closer to the Mexican earth and to the indigenes than to Spain, notwithstanding modern insistence on the Latin in Latin-American culture.

The Spaniards, through Mexico, have had an abiding influence on the architecture and language of the Southwest. They gave us our most distinctive occupation, ranching on the open range. They influenced mining greatly, and our land titles and irrigation laws still go back to Spanish and Mexican sources. After more than a hundred years of occupation of Texas and almost that length of time in other parts of the Southwest, the English-speaking Americans still have the rich accumulations of lore pertaining to coyotes, mesquites, prickly pear, and many other plants and animals to learn from the Mexicans, who got their lore partly from intimate living with nature but largely through Indian ancestry.

See "Fighting Texians," "Santa Fe and the Santa Fe Trail."

AIKEN, RILEY. "A Pack Load of Mexican Tales," in *Puro Mexicano,* published by Texas Folklore Society, 1935. Now published by Southern Methodist University Press, Dallas. Delightful.

ALEXANDER, FRANCES (and others). *Mother Goose on the Rio Grande,* Banks Upshaw, Dallas, 1944. Charming rhymes in both Spanish and English in charming form.

APPLEGATE, FRANK G. *Native Tales of New Mexico,* Philadelphia, 1932. Delicious; the real thing. OP.

ATHERTON, GERTRUDE. *The Splendid Idle Forties,* New York, 1902. Romance of Mexican California.

AUSTIN, MARY. *One-Smoke Stories,* Boston, 1934. Short tales of Spanish-speaking New Mexicans, also of Indians.

BANDELIER, A. F. *The Gilded Man,* New York, 1873. The dream of El Dorado.

BARCA, MADAM CALDERON DE LA. *Life in Mexico,* 1843; reprinted by Dutton about 1930. Among books on Mexican life to be ranked first both in readability and revealing qualities.

BELL, HORACE. *On the Old West Coast,* New York, 1930. A golden treasury of anecdotes. OP.

BENTLEY, HAROLD W. *A Dictionary of Spanish Terms in English,* New York, 1932. In a special way this book reveals the Spanish-Mexican influence on life in the Southwest; it also guides to books in English that reflect this influence. OP.

BISHOP, MORRIS. *The Odyssey of Cabeza de Vaca,* New York, 1933. Better written than Cabeza de Vaca's own narrative. OP.

BLANCO, ANTONIO FIERRO DE. *The Journey of the Flame,* Boston, 1933. Bully and flavorsome; the Californias. OP.

BOLTON, HERBERT E. *Spanish Exploration in the Southwest,* 1916. The cream of explorer narratives, well edited. *Coronado on the Turquoise Trail* (originally published in New York, 1949, under the title *Coronado: Knight of Pueblos and Plains*; now issued by University of New Mexico Press, Albuquerque). By his own work and by directing other scholars, Dr. Bolton has surpassed all other American historians of his time in output on Spanish-American history. *Coronado* is the climax of his many volumes. Its fault is being too worshipful of everything Spanish and too uncritical. A little essay on Coronado in Haniel Long's *Piñon Country* goes a good way to put this belegended figure into proper perspective.

BRENNER, ANITA. *Idols Behind Altars,* 1929. OP. The pagan worship that endures among Mexican Indians. *The Wind that Swept Mexico: The History of the Mexican Revolution, 1910-1942,* 1943, OP. *Your Mexican Holiday,* revised 1947. No writer on modern Mexico has a clearer eye or clearer intellect than Anita Brenner; she maintains good humor in her realism and never lapses into phony romance.

CABEZA DE VACA's *Narrative.* Any translation procurable. One is included in *Spanish Explorers in the Southern United States,* edited by F. W. Hodge and T. H. Lewis, now published by Barnes & Noble, New York.

The most dramatic and important aftermath of Cabeza de Vaca's twisted walk across the continent was Coronado's search for the Seven Cities of Cíbola. Coronado's precursor was Fray Marcos de Niza. *The Journey of Fray Marcos de Niza,* by Cleve Hallenbeck, with illustrations and decorations by José Cisneros, is one of the most beautiful books in format published in America. It was designed and printed by Carl Hertzog of El Paso, printer without peer between the Atlantic and the Pacific, and is issued by Southern Methodist University Press, Dallas.

CASTAÑEDA's narrative of Coronado's expedition. Winship's translation is preferred. It is included in *Spanish Explorers in the Southern United States,* cited above.

CATHER, WILLA. *Death Comes for the Archbishop,* Knopf, New York, 1927. Classical historical fiction on New Mexico.

CUMBERLAND, CHARLES C. *Mexican Revolution: Genesis under Madero,* University of Texas Press, Austin, 1952. Bibliography. To know Mexico and Mexicans without knowing anything about Mexican revolutions is like knowing the

United States in ignorance of frontiers, constitutions, and corporations. The Madero revolution that began in 1910 is still going on. Mr. Cumberland's solid book, independent in itself, is to be followed by two other volumes.

DE SOTO. Hernando de Soto made his expedition from Florida north and west at the time Coronado was exploring north and east. *The Florida of the Inca,* by Garcilaso de la Vega, translated by John and Jeannette Varner, University of Texas Press, Austin, 1951, is the first complete publishing in English of this absorbing narrative.

DÍAZ, BERNAL. *History of the Conquest.* There are several translations. A book of gusto and humanity as enduring as the results of the Conquest itself.

DOBIE, J. FRANK. *Coronado's Children,* 1930. Legendary tales of the Southwest, many of them derived from Mexican sources. *Tongues of the Monte,* 1935. A pattern of the soil of northern Mexico and its folk. *Apache Gold and Yaqui Silver,* 1939. Lost mines and money in Mexico and New Mexico. Last two books published by Little, Brown, Boston.

DOMENECH, ABBÉ. *Missionary Adventures in Texas and Mexico,* London, 1858. Delightful folklore, though Domenech would not have so designated his accounts.

FERGUSSON, HARVEY. *Blood of the Conquerors,* 1921. Fiction. OP. *Rio Grande,* Knopf, New York, 1933. Best interpretations yet written of upper Mexican class.

FLANDRAU, CHARLES M. *Viva Mexico!* New York, 1909; reissued, 1951. Delicious autobiographic narrative of life in Mexico.

FULTON, MAURICE G., and HORGAN, PAUL (editors). *New Mexico's Own Chronicle,* Dallas, 1937. OP. Selections from writers about the New Mexico scene.

GILPATRICK, WALLACE. *The Man Who Likes Mexico,* New York, 1911. OP. Bully reading.

GONZÁLEZ, JOVITA. Tales about Texas-Mexican vaquero folk in *Texas and Southwestern Lore,* in *Man, Bird, and Beast,* and in *Mustangs and Cow Horses,* Publications VI, VIII, and XVI of Texas Folklore Society.

José Cisneros: Fray Marcos, in *The Journey of Fray Marcos de Niza* by Cleve Hallenbeck (1949)

GRAHAM, R. B. CUNNINGHAME. *Hernando De Soto,* London, 1912. Biography. OP.

HARTE, BRET. *The Bell Ringer of Angels* and other legendary tales of California.

LAUGHLIN, RUTH. *Caballeros.* When the book was published in 1931, the author was named Ruth Laughlin Barker; after she discarded the Barker part, it was reissued, in 1946, by Caxton, Caldwell, Idaho. Delightful picturings of Mexican — or Spanish, as many New Mexicans prefer — life around Santa Fe.

LEA, TOM. *The Brave Bulls.* See under "Fiction."

LUMMIS, C. F. *Flowers of Our Lost Romance,* Boston, 1929. Humanistic essays on Spanish contributions to southwestern civilization. OP. *The Land of Poco Tiempo,* New York, 1913 (reissued by University of New Mexico Press, 1952), in an easier style. *A New Mexico David,* 1891, 1930. Folk tales and sketches. OP.

MERRIAM, CHARLES. *Machete,* Dallas, 1932. Plain and true to the *gente.* OP.

NIGGLI, JOSEPHINA. *Mexican Village,* University of North Carolina Press, Chapel Hill, 1945. A collection of skilfully told stories that reveal Mexican life.

O'SHAUGHNESSY, EDITH. *A Diplomat's Wife in Mexico,* New York, 1916; *Diplomatic Days,* 1917; *Intimate Pages of Mexican History,* 1920. Books of passion and power and high literary merit, interpretative of revolutionary Mexico. OP.

OTERO, NINA. *Old Spain in Our Southwest,* New York, 1936. Genuine. OP.

PORTER, KATHERINE ANNE. *Flowering Judas.* See under "Fiction."

PRESCOTT, WILLIAM H. *Conquest of Mexico.* History that is literature.

REMINGTON, FREDERIC W. *Pony Tracks,* New York, 1895. Includes sketches of Mexican ranch life.

ROSS, PATRICIA FENT. *Made in Mexico: The Story of a Country's Arts and Crafts,* Knopf, New York, 1952. Picturesquely and instructively illustrated by Carlos Merida.

TANNENBAUM, FRANK. *Peace by Revolution,* Columbia University Press, New York, 1933; *Mexico: The Struggle for Peace and Bread,* Knopf, New York, 1950. Tannenbaum dodges nothing, not even the church.

Terry's Guide to Mexico. It has everything.

Texas Folklore Society. Its publications are a storehouse of Mexican folklore in the Southwest and in Mexico also. Especially recommended are *Texas and Southwestern Lore* (VI), *Man, Bird, and Beast* (VIII), *Southwestern Lore* (IX), *Spur-of-the-Cock* (XI), *Puro Mexicano* (XII), *Texian Stomping Grounds* (XVII), *Mexican Border Ballads and Other Lore* (XXI), *The Healer of Los Olmos and Other Mexican Lore* (XXIV, 1951). All published by Southern Methodist University Press, Dallas.

TOOR, FRANCES. *A Treasury of Mexican Folkways,* Crown, New York, 1947. An anthology of life.

TURNER, TIMOTHY G. *Bullets, Bottles and Gardenias,* Dallas, 1935. Obscurely published but one of the best books on Mexican life. OP.

7

Flavor of France

THERE IS little justification for including Louisiana as a part of the Southwest. Despite the fact that the French flag—tied to a pole in Louisiana—once waved over Texas, French influence on it and other parts of the Southwest has been minor.

ARTHUR, STANLEY CLISBY. *Jean Laffite, Gentleman Rover* (1952) and *Audubon: An Intimate Life of the American Woodsman* (1937), both published by Harmanson—Publisher and Bookseller, 333 Royal St., New Orleans.

CABLE, GEORGE W. *Old Creole Days: Strange True Stories of Louisiana.*

CHOPIN, KATE. *Bayou Folk.*

FORTIER, ALCEE. Any of his work on Louisiana.

HEARN, LAFCADIO. *Chita.* A lovely story.

JOUTEL. *Journal* of La Salle's career in Texas.

KANE, HARNETT T. *Plantation Parade: The Grand Manner in Louisiana* (1945), *Natchez on the Mississippi* (1947), *Queen New Orleans* (1949), all published by Morrow, New York.

KING, GRACE. *New Orleans: The Place and the People; Balcony Stories.*

McVOY, LIZZIE CARTER. *Louisiana in the Short Story,* Louisiana State University Press, 1940.

SAXON, LYLE. *Fabulous New Orleans; Old Louisiana; Lafitte the Pirate.*

8

Backwoods Life and Humor

THE SETTLERS who put their stamp on Texas were predominantly from the southern states—and far more of them came to Texas to work out of debt than came with riches in the form of slaves. The plantation owner came too, but the go-ahead Crockett kind of backwoodsman was typical. The southern type never became so prominent in New Mexico, Arizona, and California as in Texas. Nevertheless, the fact glares out that the code of conduct—the riding and shooting tradition, the eagerness to stand up and fight for one's rights, the readiness to back one's judgment with a gun, a bowie knife, money, life itself—that characterized the whole West as well as the Southwest was southern, hardly at all New England.

The very qualities that made many of the Texas pioneers rebels to society and forced not a few of them to quit it between sun and sun without leaving new addresses fitted them to conquer the wilderness—qualities of daring, bravery, reckless abandon, heavy self-assertiveness. A lot of them were hell-raisers, for they had a lust for life and were maddened by tame respectability. Nobody but obsequious politicians and priggish "Daughters" wants to make them out as models of virtue and conformity. A smooth and settled society—a society shockingly tame—may accept Cardinal Newman's definition, "A gentleman is one who never gives offense." Under this definition a shaded violet, a butterfly, and a floating summer cloud are all gentlemen. "The art of war," said Napoleon, "is to make offense." Conquering the hostile Texas wilderness meant war with nature and against savages as well as against Mexicans. Go-ahead Crockett's ideal of a gentleman was one who looked in another direction while a visitor was pouring himself out a horn of whiskey.

Laying aside climatic influences on occupations and manners, certain Spanish influences, and minor Pueblo Indian touches, the Southwest from the point of view of the bedrock Anglo-Saxon character that has made it might well include Arkansas and Missouri. The realism of southern folk and of a very considerable body of indigenous literature representing them has been too much overshadowed by a kind of *So Red the Rose* idealization of slave-holding aristocrats.

ALLSOPP, FRED W. *Folklore of Romantic Arkansas,* 2 vols., Grolier Society, 1931. Allsopp assembled a rich and varied collection of materials in the tone of "The Arkansas Traveler." OP.

ARRINGTON, ALFRED W. *The Rangers and Regulators of the Tanaha,* 1856. East Texas bloodletting.

BALDWIN, JOSEPH G. *The Flush Times of Alabama and Mississippi,* 1853.

BLAIR, WALTER. *Horse Sense in American Humor from Benjamin Franklin to Ogden Nash,* 1942. OP. *Native American Humor,* 1937. OP. *Tall Tale America,* Coward-McCann, New York, 1944. Orderly analyses with many concrete examples. With Franklin J. Meine as co-author, *Mike Fink, King of Mississippi River Keelboatmen,* 1933. Biography of a folk type against pioneer and frontier background. OP.

BOATRIGHT, MODY C. *Folk Laughter on the American Frontier.* See under "Interpreters."

CLARK, THOMAS D. *The Rampaging Frontier,* 1939. OP. Historical picturization and analysis, fortified by incidents and tales of "Varmints," "Liars," "Quarter Horses," "Fiddlin'," "Foolin' with the Gals," etc.

CROCKETT, DAVID. *Autobiography.* Reprinted many times. Scribner's edition in the "Modern Students' Library" includes *Colonel Crockett's Exploits and Adventures in*

Texas. Crockett set the backwoods type. See treatment of him in Parrington's *Main Currents in American Thought.* Richard M. Dorson's *Davy Crockett, American Comic Legend,* 1939, is a summation of the Crockett tradition.

FEATHERSTONHAUGH, G. W. *Excursion through the Slave States,* London, 1866. Refreshing on manners and characters.

FLACK, CAPTAIN. *The Texas Ranger, or Real Life in the Backwoods,* London, 1866.

GERSTAECKER, FREDERICK. *Wild Sports in the Far West.* Nothing better on backwoods life in the Mississippi Valley.

HAMMETT, SAMUEL ADAMS (who wrote under the name of Philip Paxton), *Piney Woods Tavern; or Sam Slick in Texas* and *A Stray Yankee in Texas.* Humor on the roughneck element. For treatment of Hammett as man and writer see *Sam Slick in Texas,* by W. Stanley Hoole, Naylor, San Antonio, 1945.

HARRIS, GEORGE W. *Sut Lovingood,* New York, 1867. Prerealism.

HOGUE, WAYMAN. *Back Yonder.* Minton, Balch, New York, 1932. Ozark life. OP.

HOOPER, J. J. *Adventures of Captain Simon Suggs,* 1845. OP. Downright realism. Like Longstreet, Hooper in maturity wanted his realism forgotten. An Alabama journalist, he got into the camp of respectable slave-holders and spent the later years of his life shouting against the "enemies of the institution of African slavery." His life partly explains the lack of intellectual honesty in most southern spokesmen today. *Alias Simon Suggs: The Life and Times of Johnson Jones Hooper,* by W. Stanley Hoole, University of Alabama Press, 1952, is a careful study of Hooper's career.

HUDSON, A. P. *Humor of the Old Deep South,* New York, 1936. An anthology. OP.

LONGSTREET, A. B. *Georgia Scenes,* 1835. Numerous reprints. Realism.

MASTERSON, JAMES R. *Tall Tales of Arkansas*, Boston, 1943. OP. The title belies this excellent social history—by a scholar. It has become quite scarce on account of the fact that it contains unexpurgated versions of the notorious speech on "Change the Name of Arkansas"—which in 1919 in officers' barracks at Bordeaux, France, I heard a lusty individual recite with as many variations as Roxane of *Cyrano de Bergerac* wanted in love-making. When Fred W. Allsopp, newspaper publisher and pillar of Arkansas respectability, found that this book of unexpurgations had been dedicated to him by the author—a Harvard Ph.D. teaching in Michigan—he almost "had a colt."

MEINE, FRANKLIN J. (editor). *Tall Tales of the Southwest*, Knopf, New York, 1930. A superbly edited and superbly selected anthology with appendices affording a guide to the whole field of early southern humor and realism. No cavalier idealism. The "Southwest" of this excellent book is South.

OLMSTED, FREDERICK LAW. *A Journey in the Seaboard Slave States*, 1856. *A Journey Through Texas*, 1857. Invaluable books on social history.

POSTL, KARL ANTON (Charles Sealsfield or Francis Hardman, pseudonyms). *The Cabin Book; Frontier Life*. Translations all OP.

RANDOLPH, VANCE. *We Always Lie to Strangers*, Columbia University Press, New York, 1951. A collection of tall tales of the adding machine variety. Fertile in invention but devoid of any yearning for the beautiful or suggestion that the human spirit hungers for something beyond horse play; in short, typical of American humor.

ROURKE, CONSTANCE. *American Humor*, 1931; *Davy Crockett*, 1934; *Roots of American Culture and Other Essays*, 1942, all published by Harcourt, Brace, New York.

THOMPSON, WILLIAM T. *Major Jones's Courtship*, Philadelphia, 1844. Realism.

THORPE, T. B. *The Hive of the Bee-Hunter*, New York, 1854. This excellent book should be reprinted.

WATTERSON, HENRY. *Oddities in Southern Life and Character*, Boston, 1882. An anthology with interpretative notes.

WILSON, CHARLES MORROW. *Backwoods America*. University of North Carolina Press, Chapel Hill, 1935. Well ordered survey with excellent samplings.

WOOD, RAY. *The American Mother Goose*, 1940; *Fun in American Folk Rhymes*, 1952; both published by Lippincott, Philadelphia.

9

How the Early Settlers Lived

DESPITE THE FACT that the tendency of a majority of early day rememberers has been to emphasize Indian fights, killings, and other sensational episodes, chronicles rich in the everyday manners and customs of the folk are plentiful. The classic of them all is Noah Smithwick's *The Evolution of a State*, listed below.

See also "Backwoods Life and Humor," "Pioneer Doctors," "Women Pioneers," "Fighting Texians."

BARKER, E. C. *The Austin Papers*. Four volumes of sources for any theme in social history connected with colonial Texans.

BATES, ED. F. *History and Reminiscences of Denton County*, Denton, Texas, 1918. A sample of much folk life found in county histories.

BELL, HORACE. *On the Old West Coast*, New York, 1930. Social history by anecdote. California. OP.

BRACHT, VIKTOR. *Texas in 1848*, translated from the German by C. F. Schmidt, San Antonio, 1931. Better on natural resources than on human inhabitants. OP.

CARL, PRINCE OF SOLMS-BRAUNFELS. *Texas, 1844-1845*. Translation, Houston, 1936. OP.

COX, C. C. "Reminiscences," in Vol. VI of *Southwestern Historical Quarterly*. One of the best of many pioneer recollections published by the Texas State Historical Association.

CROCKETT, DAVID. Anything about him.

DICK, EVERETT. *The Sod House Frontier* (1937) and *Vanguards of the Frontier* (1941). Both OP. Life on northern Plains into Rocky Mountains, but applicable to life southward.

DOBIE, J. FRANK. *The Flavor of Texas*, 1936. OP. Considerable social history.

FENLEY, FLORENCE. *Oldtimers: Their Own Stories*, Uvalde, Texas, 1939. OP. Faithful reporting of realistic detail. Southwest Texas, mostly ranch life.

FRANTZ, JOE B. *Gail Borden, Dairyman to a Nation*. University of Oklahoma Press, Norman, 1951. This biography of a newspaperman and inventor brings out sides of pioneer life that emphasis on fighting, farming, and ranching generally overlooks.

GERSTAECKER, FREDERICK. *Wild Sports in the Far West*, 1860. Dances are among the sports.

HARRIS, MRS. DILUE. "Reminiscences," edited by Mrs. A. B. Looscan, in Vols. IV and VII of *Southwestern Historical Quarterly*.

HART, JOHN A. *History of Pioneer Days in Texas and Oklahoma;* no date. Extended and republished under the title of *Pioneer Days in the Southwest*, 1909. Much on frontier ways of living.

HOFF, CAROL. *Johnny Texas*, Wilcox and Follett, Chicago, 1950. Juvenile, historical fiction. Delightful in both text and illustrations.

HOGAN, WILLIAM R. *The Texas Republic: A Social and Economic History*, University of Oklahoma Press, 1946. Long on facts, short on intellectual activity; that is, on interpretations from the perspective of time and civilization.

HOLDEN, W. C. *Alkali Trails*, Dallas, 1930. Pioneer life in West Texas. OP.

HOLLEY, MARY AUSTIN. *Texas . . . in a Series of Letters*, Baltimore, 1833; reprinted under the title of *Letters of an American Traveler*, edited by Mattie Austin Hatcher, Dallas, 1933. First good book on Texas to be printed. OP.

Lamar Papers. Six volumes of scrappy source material on Texas history and life, issued by Texas State Library, Austin. OP.

LEWIS, WILLIE NEWBURY. *Between Sun and Sod*, Clarendon, Texas, 1938. OP. Again, want of perspective.

LUBBOCK, F. R. *Six Decades in Texas*, Austin, 1900.

McCONNELL, H. H. *Five Years a Cavalryman*, Jacksboro, Texas, 1889. Bully.

McDANIELD, H. F., and TAYLOR, NATHANIEL A. *The Coming Empire, or 2000 Miles in Texas on Horseback*, New York, 1878; privately reprinted, 1937. Delightful travel narrative. OP.

McNEAL, T. A. *When Kansas Was Young*, New York, 1922. Episodes and characters of Plains country. OP.

OLMSTED, FREDERICK LAW. *A Journey Through Texas*, New York, 1857. Olmsted journeyed in order to see. He saw.

READ, OPIE. *An Arkansas Planter*, 1896. Pleasant fiction.

RICHARDSON, ALBERT D. *Beyond the Mississippi*, Hartford, 1867. What a traveling journalist saw.

RISTER, CARL C. *Southern Plainsmen*, University of Oklahoma Press, 1938. Though pedestrian in style, good social data. Bibliography.

ROEMER, DR. FERDINAND. *Texas*, translated from the German by Oswald Mueller, San Antonio, 1935. OP. Roemer, a geologist, rode through Texas in the forties and made acute observations on the land, its plants and animals, and the settlers.

SCHMITZ, JOSEPH WILLIAM. *Thus They Lived*, Naylor, San Antonio, 1935. This would have been a good social history of Texas had the writer devoted ten more years to the subject. Unsatisfactory bibliography.

SHIPMAN, DANIEL. *Frontier Life, 58 Years in Texas*, n.p., 1879. One of the pioneer reminiscences that should be reprinted.

SMITH, HENRY. "Reminiscences," in *Southwestern Historical Quarterly*, Vol. XIV. Telling details.

SMITHWICK, NOAH. *The Evolution of a State*, Austin, 1900. Reprinted by Steck, Austin, 1935. Best of all books dealing with life in early Texas. Bully reading.

Southwestern Historical Quarterly, published since 1897 by Texas State Historical Association, Austin. A depository of all kinds of history; the first twenty-five or thirty volumes are the more interesting.

SWEET, ALEXANDER E., and KNOX, J. ARMOY. *On a Mexican Mustang Through Texas,* Hartford, 1883. Humorous satire, often penetrating and ruddy with actuality.

WALLIS, JONNIE LOCKHART. *Sixty Years on the Brazos: The Life and Letters of Dr. John Washington Lockhart,* privately printed, Los Angeles, 1930. In notebook style, but as rare in essence as it is among dealers in out-of-print books.

WAUGH, JULIA NOTT. *Castroville and Henry Castro,* San Antonio, 1934. OP. Best-written monograph dealing with any aspect of Texas history that I have read.

WYNN, AFTON. "Pioneer Folk Ways," in *Straight Texas,* Texas Folklore Society Publication XIII, 1937.

10

Fighting Texians

THE TEXAS PEOPLE belong to a fighting tradition that the majority of them are proud of. The footholds that the Spaniards and Mexicans held in Texas were maintained by virtue of fighting, irrespective of missionary baptizing. The purpose of the Anglo-American colonizer Stephen F. Austin to "redeem Texas from the wilderness" was accomplished only by fighting. The Texans bought their liberty with blood and maintained it for nine years as a republic with blood. It was fighting men who pushed back the frontiers and blazed trails.

The fighting tradition is now giving way to the oil tradition. The Texas myth as imagined by non-Texans is coming to embody oil millionaires in airplanes instead of horsemen with six-shooters and rifles. See Edna Ferber's *Giant* (1952 novel). Nevertheless, many Texans who never rode a horse over three miles at a stretch wear cowboy boots, and a lot of Texans are under the delusion that bullets and atomic bombs can settle complexities that demand informed intelligence and the power to think.

As I have pointed out in *The Flavor of Texas*, the chronicles of men who fought the Mexicans and were prisoners to them comprise a unique unit in the personal narratives and annals of America.

Many of the books listed under the headings of "Texas Rangers," "How the Early Settlers Lived," and "Range Life" specify the fighting tradition.

BEAN, PETER ELLIS. *Memoir,* published first in Vol. I of Yoakum's *History of Texas;* in 1930 printed as a small book by the Book Club of Texas, Dallas, now OP. A fascinating narrative.

BECHDOLT, FREDERICK R. *Tales of the Old Timers,* New York, 1924. Forceful retelling of the story of the Mier Expedition and of other activities of the "fighting Texans." OP.

CHABOT, FREDERICK C. *The Perote Prisoners,* San Antonio, 1934. Annotated diaries of Texas prisoners in Mexico. OP.

DOBIE, J. FRANK. *The Flavor of Texas,* Dallas, 1936. OP. Chapters on Bean, Green, Duval, Kendall, and other representers of the fighting Texans.

DUVAL, JOHN C. *Adventures of Bigfoot Wallace,* 1870; *Early Times in Texas,* 1892. Both books are kept in print by Steck, Austin. For biography and critical estimate, see *John C. Duval: First Texas Man of Letters,* by J. Frank Dobie (illustrated by Tom Lea), Dallas, 1939. OP. *Early Times in Texas,* called "the *Robinson Crusoe* of Texas," is Duval's story of the Goliad Massacre and of his escape from it. Duval served as a Texas Ranger with Bigfoot Wallace, who was in the Mier Expedition. His narrative of Bigfoot's *Adventures* is the rollickiest and the most flavorsome that any American frontiersman has yet inspired. The tiresome thumping on the hero theme present in many biographies of frontiersmen is entirely absent. Stanley Vestal wrote *Bigfoot Wallace* also, Boston, 1942. OP.

ERATH, MAJOR GEORGE G. *Memoirs,* Texas State Historical Association, Austin, 1923. Erath understood his fellow Texians. OP.

GILLETT, JAMES B. *Six Years with the Texas Rangers,* 1921. OP.

GREEN, THOMAS JEFFERSON. *Journal of the Texan Expedition against Mier,* 1845; reprinted by Steck, Austin, 1936. Green was one of the leaders of the Mier Expedition. He lived in wrath and wrote with fire. For information on Green see *Recollections and Reflections* by his son, Wharton J. Green, 1906. OP.

HOUSTON, SAM. *The Raven,* by Marquis James, 1929, is

not the only biography of the Texan general, but it is the best, and embodies most of what has been written on Houston —excepting the multivolumed *Houston Papers* issued by the University of Texas Press, Austin, under the editorship of E. C. Barker. Houston was an original character even after he became a respectable Baptist.

KENDALL, GEORGE W. *Narrative of the Texan Santa Fe Expedition,* 1844; reprinted by Steck, Austin, 1936. Two volumes. Kendall, a New Orleans journalist in search of copy, joined the Santa Fe Expedition sent by the Republic of Texas to annex New Mexico. Lost on the Staked Plains and then marched afoot as a prisoner to Mexico City, he found plenty of copy and wrote a narrative that if it were not so journalistically verbose might rank alongside Dana's *Two Years Before the Mast.* Fayette Copeland's *Kendall of the Picayune,* 1943 but OP, is a biography. An interesting parallel to Kendall's *Narrative* is *Letters and Notes on the Texan Santa Fe Expedition, 1841-1842,* by Thomas Falconer, with Notes and Introduction by F. W. Hodge, New York, 1930. OP. The route of the expedition is logged and otherwise illuminated in *The Texan Santa Fe Trail,* by H. Bailey Carroll, Panhandle-Plains Historical Society, Canyon, Texas, 1951.

LEACH, JOSEPH. *The Typical Texan: Biography of an American Myth,* Southern Methodist University Press, Dallas, 1952. At the time Texas was emerging, the three main types of Americans were Yankees, southern aristocrats, Kentucky westerners embodied by Daniel Boone. Texas took over the Kentucky tradition. It was enlarged by Crockett, who stayed in Texas only long enough to get killed, Sam Houston, and Bigfoot Wallace. Novels, plays, stories, travel books, and the Texans themselves have kept the tradition going. This is the main thesis of the book. Mr. Leach fails to note that the best books concerning Texas have done little to keep the typical Texan alive and that a great part of the present Texas Brags spirit is as absurdly unrealistic as Mussolini's splurge at making twentieth-century Italians imagine themselves a

John W. Thomason, in his *Lone Star Preacher* (1941)

reincarnation of Caesar's Roman legions. Mr. Leach dissects the myth and then swallows it.

LINN, JOHN J. *Reminiscences of Fifty Years in Texas*, 1883; reprinted by Steck, Austin, 1936. Mixture of personal narrative and historical notes, written with energy and prejudice.

MAVERICK, MARY A. *Memoirs*, 1921. OP. Mrs. Maverick's husband, Sam Maverick, was among the citizens of San Antonio haled off to Mexico as prisoners in 1842.

MORRELL, Z. N. *Fruits and Flowers in the Wilderness*, 1872. OP. Morrell, a circuit-riding Baptist preacher, fought the Indians and the Mexicans. See other books of this kind listed under "Circuit Riders and Missionaries."

PERRY, GEORGE SESSIONS. *Texas, A World in Itself,* McGraw-Hill, New York, 1942. Especially good chapter on the Alamo.

SMYTHE, H. *Historical Sketch of Parker County, Texas,* 1877. One of various good county histories of Texas replete with fighting. For bibliography of this extensive class of literature consult *Texas County Histories,* by H. Bailey Carroll, Texas State Historical Association, Austin, 1943. OP.

SONNICHSEN, C. L. *I'll Die Before I'll Run: The Story of the Great Feuds of Texas*—and of some not great. Harper, New York, 1951.

SOWELL, A. J. *Rangers and Pioneers of Texas,* 1884; *Life of Bigfoot Wallace,* 1899; *Early Settlers and Indian Fighters of Southwest Texas,* 1900. All OP; all meaty with the character of ready-to-fight but peace-seeking Texas pioneers. Sowell will some day be recognized as an extraordinary chronicler.

STAPP, WILLIAM P. *The Prisoners of Perote,* 1845; reprinted by Steck, Austin, 1936. Journal of one of the Mier men who drew a white bean.

THOMASON, JOHN W. *Lone Star Preacher,* Scribner's, New York, 1941. The cream, the essence, the spirit, and the body of the fighting tradition of Texas. Historical novel of Civil War.

WEBB, WALTER PRESCOTT. *The Texas Rangers,* Houghton Mifflin, Boston, 1935. See under "Texas Rangers."

WILBARGER, J. W. *Indian Depredations in Texas,* 1889; reprinted by Steck, Austin, 1936. Narratives that have for generations been a household heritage among Texas families who fought for their land.

11

Texas Rangers

THE TEXAS RANGERS were never more than a handful in number, but they were picked men who knew how to ride, shoot, and tell the truth. On the Mexican border and on the Indian frontier, a few rangers time and again proved themselves more effective than battalions of soldiers.

> Oh, pray for the ranger, you kind-hearted stranger,
>   He has roamed over the prairies for many a year;
> He has kept the Comanches from off your ranches,
>   And chased them far over the Texas frontier.

BANTA, WILLIAM. *Twenty-seven Years on the Texas Frontier,* 1893; reprinted, 1933. OP.

GAY, BEATRICE GRADY. *Into the Setting Sun,* Santa Anna, Texas, 1936. Coleman County scenes and characters, dominated by ranger character. OP.

GILLETT, JAMES B. *Six Years with the Texas Rangers,* printed for the author at Austin, Texas, 1921. He paid the printer cash for either one or two thousand copies, as he told me, and sold them personally. Edited by Milo M. Quaife, the book was published by Yale University Press in 1925. This edition was reprinted, 1943, by the Lakeside Press, Chicago, in its "Lakeside Classics" series, which are given away by the publishers at Christmas annually and are not for sale — except through second-hand dealers. Meantime, in 1927, the narrative had appeared under title of *The Texas Ranger,* "in collaboration with Howard R. Driggs," a professional neutralizer for school readers of any writing not standardized, published by World Book Co., Yonkers-on-Hudson, New

York. All editions OP. I regard Gillett as the strongest and straightest of all ranger narrators. He combined in his nature wild restlessness and loyal gentleness. He wrote in sunlight.

GREER, JAMES K. *Buck Barry*, Dallas, 1932. OP. *Colonel Jack Hays, Texas Frontier Leader and California Builder*, Dutton, New York, 1952. Hays achieved more vividness in reputation than narratives about him have attained to.

JENNINGS, N. A. *The Texas Ranger*, New York, 1899; reprinted 1930, with foreword by J. Frank Dobie. OP. Good narrative.

MALTBY, W. JEFF. *Captain Jeff*, Colorado, Texas, 1906. Amorphous. OP.

MARTIN, JACK. *Border Boss*, San Antonio, 1942. Mediocre biography of Captain John R. Hughes. OP.

PAINE, ALBERT BIGELOW. *Captain Bill McDonald*, New York, 1909. Paine did not do so well by "Captain Bill" as he did in his rich biography of Mark Twain. OP.

PIKE, JAMES. *Scout and Ranger*, 1865, reprinted 1932 by Princeton University Press. Pike drew a long bow; interesting. OP.

RAYMOND, DORA NEILL. *Captain Lee Hall of Texas*, Norman, Oklahoma, 1940. OP.

REID, SAMUEL C. *Scouting Expeditions of the Texas Rangers*, 1859; reprinted by Steck, Austin, 1936. Texas Rangers in Mexican War.

ROBERTS, DAN W. *Rangers and Sovereignty*, 1914. OP. Roberts was better as ranger than as writer.

ROBERTS, MRS. D. W. (wife of Captain Dan W. Roberts). *A Woman's Reminiscences of Six Years in Camp with The Texas Rangers*, Austin, 1928. OP. Mrs. Roberts was a sensible and charming woman with a seeing eye.

SOWELL, A. J. *Rangers and Pioneers of Texas*, San Antonio, 1884. A graphic book down to bedrock. OP.

WEBB, WALTER PRESCOTT. *The Texas Rangers*, Houghton Mifflin, Boston, 1935. The beginning, middle, and end of the subject. Bibliography.

12

Women Pioneers

ONE REASON for the ebullience of life and rollicky careless-
ness on the frontiers of the West was the lack—temporary—
of women. The men, mostly young, had given no hostages to
fortune. They were generally as free from family cares as the
buccaneers. This was especially true of the first ranches on
the Great Plains, of cattle trails, of mining camps, logging
camps, and of trapping expeditions. It was not true of the
colonial days in Texas, of ranch life in the southern part of
Texas, of homesteading all over the West, of emigrant trails
to California and Oregon, of backwoods life.

Various items listed under "How the Early Settlers
Lived" contain material on pioneer women.

ALDERSON, NANNIE T., and SMITH, HELENA HUNT-
INGTON. *A Bride Goes West,* New York, 1942. Montana in
the eighties. OP.

BAKER, D. W. C. *A Texas Scrapbook,* 1875; reprinted,
1936, by Steck, Austin.

BROTHERS, MARY HUDSON. *A Pecos Pioneer,* 1943. OP.
The best part of this book is not about the writer's brother,
who cowboyed with Chisum's Jinglebob outfit and ran into
Billy the Kid, but is Mary Hudson's own life. Only Ross
Santee has equaled her in description of drought and rain.
The last chapters reveal a girl's inner life, amid outward expe-
riences, as no other woman's chronicle of ranch ways—sheep
ranch here.

CALL, HUGHIE. *Golden Fleece,* Houghton Mifflin, Boston, 1942. Hughie Call became wife of a Montana sheepman early in this century. OP.

CLEAVELAND, AGNES MORLEY. *No Life for a Lady,* Houghton Mifflin, Boston, 1941. Bright, witty, penetrating; anecdotal. Best account of frontier life from woman's point of view yet published. New Mexico is the setting, toward turn of the century. People who wished Mrs. Cleaveland would write another book were disappointed when her *Satan's Paradise* appeared in 1952.

ELLIS, ANNE. *The Life of An Ordinary Woman,* 1929, and *Plain Anne Ellis,* 1931, both OP. Colorado country and town. Books of disillusioned observations, wit, and wisdom by a frank woman.

FAUNCE, HILDA. *Desert Wife,* 1934. OP. Desert loneliness at a Navajo trading post.

HARRIS, MRS. DILUE. "Reminiscences," in *Southwestern Historical Quarterly,* Vols. IV and VII.

KLEBERG, ROSA. "Early Experiences in Texas," in *Quarterly of the Texas State Historical Association* (initial title for *Southwestern Historical Quarterly*), Vols. I and II.

MAGOFFIN, SUSAN SHELBY. *Down the Santa Fe Trail,* 1926. OP. She was juicy and a bride, and all life was bright to her.

MATTHEWS, SALLIE REYNOLDS. *Interwoven,* Houston, 1936. Ranch life in the Texas frontier as a refined and intelligent woman saw it. OP.

MAVERICK, MARY A. *Memoirs,* San Antonio, 1921. OP. Essential.

PICKRELL, ANNIE DOOM. *Pioneer Women in Texas,* Austin, 1929. Too much lady business but valuable. OP.

POE, SOPHIE A. *Buckboard Days,* edited by Eugene Cunningham, Caldwell, Idaho, 1936. Mrs. Poe was there—New Mexico.

RAK, MARY KIDDER. *A Cowman's Wife,* Houghton Mifflin, Boston, 1934. The external experiences of an ex-teacher on a small Arizona ranch.

RHODES, MAY D. *The Hired Man on Horseback,* 1938. Biography of Eugene Manlove Rhodes, but also warm-natured autobiography of the woman who ranched with "Gene" in New Mexico. OP.

RICHARDS, CLARICE E. *A Tenderfoot Bride,* Garden City, N. Y., 1920. OP. Charming.

STEWART, ELINOR P. *Letters of a Woman Homesteader,* Boston, 1914. OP.

WHITE, OWEN P. *A Frontier Mother,* New York, 1929. OP. Overdone, as White overdid every subject he touched.

WILBARGER, J. W. *Indian Depredations in Texas,* 1889; reprinted by Steck, Austin, 1936. A glimpse into the lives led by families that gave many women to savages—for death or for Cynthia Ann Parker captivity.

WYNN, AFTON. "Pioneer Folk Ways," in *Straight Texas,* Texas Folklore Society Publication XIII, 1937. Excellent.

13

Circuit Riders and Missionaries

NOTWITHSTANDING both the tradition and the facts of hard-shooting, hard-riding cowboys, of bad men, of border lawlessness, of inhabitants who had left some other place under a cloud, of frontier towns "west of God," hard layouts and conscienceless "courthouse crowds" — notwithstanding all this, the Southwest has been and is religious-minded. This is not to say that it is spiritual-natured. It belongs to H. L. Mencken's "Bible Belt." "Pass-the-Biscuits" Pappy O'Daniel got to be governor of Texas and then U.S. senator by advertising his piety. A politician as "ignorant as a Mexican hog" on foreign affairs and the complexities of political economy can run in favor of what he and the voters call religion and leave an informed man of intellect and sincerity in the shade. The biggest campmeeting in the Southwest, the Bloys Campmeeting near Fort Davis, Texas, is in the midst of an enormous range country away from all factories and farmers.

Since about 1933 the United States Indian Service has not only allowed but rather encouraged the Indians to revert to their own religious ceremonies. They have always been religious. The Spanish colonists of the Southwest, as elsewhere, were zealously Catholic, and their descendants have generally remained Catholic. The first English-speaking settlers of the region—the colonists led by Stephen F. Austin to Texas— were overwhelmingly Protestant, though in order to establish Mexican citizenship and get titles to homestead land they had, technically, to declare themselves Catholics. One of the causes of the Texas Revolution as set forth by the Texans in their Declaration of Independence was the Mexican government's denial of "the right of worshipping the Almighty according to the dictates of our own conscience." A history of southwestern society that left out the Bible would be as badly gapped as one leaving out the horse or the six-shooter.

See chapter entitled "On the Lord's Side" in Dobie's *The Flavor of Texas*. Most of the books listed under "How the Early Settlers Lived" contain information on religion and preachers. Church histories are about as numerous as state histories. Virtually all county histories take into account church development. The books listed below are strong on personal experiences.

ASBURY, FRANCIS. Three or more lives have been written of this representative pioneer bishop.

BOLTON, HERBERT E. *The Padre on Horseback,* 1932. Life of the Jesuit missionary Kino. OP.

BROWNLOW, W. G. *Portrait and Biography of Parson Brownlow, the Tennessee Patriot,* 1862. Brownlow was a very representative figure. Under the title of *William G. Brownlow, Fighting Parson of the Southern Highland,* E. M. Coulter has brought out a thorough life of him, published by University of North Carolina Press, Chapel Hill, 1937.

BURLESON, RUFUS C. *Life and Writings,* 1901. OP. The autobiographical 'part of this amorphously arranged volume is a social document of the first rank.

CARTWRIGHT, PETER. *Autobiography,* 1857. Out of Kentucky, into Indiana and then into Illinois, where he ran against Lincoln for Congress, Cartwright rode with saddlebags and Bible. Sandburg characterizes him as "an enemy of whisky, gambling, jewelry, fine clothes, and higher learning." He seems to me more unlovely in his intolerance and sectarianism than most circuit riders of the Southwest, but as a militant, rough-and-ready "soldier of the Lord" he represented southwestern frontiers as well as his own.

CRANFILL, J. B. *Chronicle, A Story of Life in Texas,* 1916. Cranfill was a lot of things besides a Baptist preacher—trail driver, fiddler, publisher, always an observer. OP.

DeVILBISS, JOHN WESLEY. *Reminiscences and Events* (compiled by H. A. Graves), 1886. The very essence of pioneering.

DOMENECH, ABBÉ. *Missionary Adventures in Texas and Mexico* (translated from the French), London, 1858. OP. The Abbé always had eyes open for wonders. He saw them. Delicious narrative.

EVANS, WILL G. *Border Skylines,* published in Dallas, 1940, for Bloys Campmeeting Association, Fort Davis, Texas. Chronicles of the men and women—cow people—and cow country responsible for the best known campmeeting, held annually, Texas has ever had. OP.

GRAVIS, PETER W. *25 Years on the Outside Row of the Northwest Texas Annual Conference,* Comanche, Texas, 1892. Another one of those small personal records, privately printed but full of juice. OP.

LIDE, ANNA A. *Robert Alexander and the Early Methodist Church in Texas,* La Grange, Texas, 1935. OP.

MORRELL, Z. N. *Fruits and Flowers in the Wilderness,* 1872. Though reprinted three times, last in 1886, long OP. In many ways the best circuit rider's chronicle of the Southwest that has been published. Morrell fought Indians and Mexicans in Texas and was rich in other experiences.

MORRIS, T. A. *Miscellany,* 1854. The "Notes of Travel" —particularly to Texas in 1841—are what makes this book interesting.

PARISOT, P. F. *Reminiscences of a Texas Missionary,* 1899. Mostly the Texas-Mexican border.

POTTER, ANDREW JACKSON, commonly called the "Fighting Parson." *Life* of him by H. A. Graves, 1890, not nearly so good as Potter was himself.

THOMASON, JOHN W. *Lone Star Preacher,* Scribner's, New York, 1941. Fiction, true to humanity. The moving story of a Texas chaplain who carried a Bible in one hand and a captain's sword in the other through the Civil War.

14

Lawyers, Politicians, J. P.'s

STEPHEN F. AUSTIN wanted to exclude lawyers, along with roving frontiersmen, from his colonies in Texas, and hoped thus to promote a utopian society. The lawyers got in, however. Their wit, the anecdotes of which they were both subject and author, and the political stories they made traditional from the stump, have not been adequately set down. As criminal lawyers they stood as high in society as corporation lawyers stand now and were a good deal more popular, though less wealthy. The code of independence that fostered personal violence and justified killings—in contradistinction to murders—and that ran to excess in outlaws naturally fostered the criminal lawyer. His type is now virtually obsolete.

Keen observers, richly stored in experience and delightful in talk, as many lawyers of the Southwest have been and are, very few of them have written on other than legal subjects. James D. Lynch's *The Bench and the Bar of Texas* (1885) is confined to the eminence of "eminent jurists" and to the mastery of "masters of jurisprudence." What we want is the flavor of life as represented by such characters as witty Three-Legged Willie (Judge R. M. Williamson) and mysterious Jonas Harrison. It takes a self-lover to write good autobiography. Lawyers are certainly as good at self-loving as preachers, but we have far better autobiographic records of circuit riders than of early-day lawyers.

Like them, the pioneer justice of peace resides more in folk anecdotes than in chroniclings. Horace Bell's expansive *On the Old West Coast* so represents him. A continent away, David Crockett, in his *Autobiography*, confessed, "I was afraid some one would ask me what the judiciary was. If I knowed I wish I may be shot." Before this, however, Crockett had been a J. P. "I gave my decisions on the principles of common justice and honesty between man and man, and relied on natural born sense, and not on law learning to guide me; for I had never read a page in a law book in all my life."

COOMBES, CHARLES E. *The Prairie Dog Lawyer*, Dallas, 1945. OP. Experiences and anecdotes by a lawyer better read in rough-and-ready humanity than in law. The prairie dogs have all been poisoned out from the West Texas country over which he ranged from court to court.

HAWKINS, WALACE. *The Case of John C. Watrous, United States Judge for Texas: A Political Story of High Crimes and Misdemeanors*, Southern Methodist University Press, Dallas, 1950. More technical than social.

KITTRELL, NORMAN G. *Governors Who Have Been and Other Public Men of Texas*, Houston, 1921. OP. Best collection of lawyer anecdotes of the Southwest.

ROBINSON, DUNCAN W. *Judge Robert McAlpin Williamson, Texas' Three-Legged Willie*, Texas State Historical Association, Austin, 1948. This was the Republic of Texas judge who laid a Colt revolver across a Bowie knife and said: "Here is the constitution that overrides the law."

SONNICHSEN, C. L. *Roy Bean, Law West of the Pecos*, Macmillan, New York, 1943. Roy Bean (1830-1903), justice of peace at Langtry, Texas, advertised himself as "Law West of the Pecos." He was more picaresque than picturesque; folk imagination gave him notoriety. The Texas State Highway Department maintains for popular edification the beer joint wherein he held court. Three books have been written about him, besides scores of newspaper and magazine articles. The only biography of validity is Sonnichsen's.

SLOAN, RICHARD E. *Memories of an Arizona Judge*, Stanford, California, 1932. Full of humanity. OP.

SMITH, E. F. *A Saga of Texas Law: A Factual Story of Texas Law, Lawyers, Judges and Famous Lawsuits*, Naylor, San Antonio, 1940. Interesting.

15

Pioneer Doctors

BEFORE the family doctors came, frontiersmen sawed off legs with handsaws, tied up arteries with horsetail hair, cauterized them with branding irons. Before homemade surgery with steel tools was practiced, Mexican *curanderas* (herb women) supplied *remedios,* and they still know the medicinal properties of every weed and bush. Herb stores in San Antonio, Brownsville, and El Paso do a thriving business. Behind the *curanderas* were the medicine men of the tribes. Not all their lore was superstition, as any one who reads the delectable autobiography of Gideon Lincecum, published by the Mississippi Historical Society in 1904, will agree. Lincecum, learned in botany, a sharply-edged individual who later moved to Texas, went out to live with a Choctaw medicine man and wrote down all his lore about the virtues of native plants. The treatise has never been printed.

The extraordinary life of Lincecum has, however, been interestingly delineated in Samuel Wood Geiser's *Naturalists of the Frontier,* Southern Methodist University Press, 1937, 1948, and in Pat Ireland Nixon's *The Medical Story of Early Texas,* listed below. No historical novelist could ask for a richer theme than Gideon Lincecum or Edmund Montgomery, the subject of I. K. Stephens' biography listed below.

BUSH, I. J. *Gringo Doctor,* Caldwell, Idaho, 1939. OP. Dr. Bush represented frontier medicine and surgery on both sides of the Rio Grande. Living at El Paso, he was for a time with the Maderistas in the revolution against Díaz.

COE, URLING C. *Frontier Doctor,* New York, 1939. OP.

Not of the Southwest but representing other frontier doctors. Lusty autobiography full of characters and anecdotes.

DODSON, RUTH. "Don Pedrito Jaramillo: The Curandero of Los Olmos," in *The Healer of Los Olmos and Other Mexican Lore* (Publication of the Texas Folklore Society XXIV), edited by Wilson M. Hudson, Southern Methodist University Press, Dallas, 1951. Don Pedrito was no more of a fraud than many an accredited psychiatrist, and he was the opposite of offensive.

NIXON, PAT IRELAND. *A Century of Medicine in San Antonio,* published by the author, San Antonio, 1936. Rich in information, diverting in anecdote, and tonic in philosophy. Bibliography. *The Medical Story of Early Texas, 1528-1835* [San Antonio], 1946. Lightness of life with scholarly thoroughness; many character sketches.

RED, MRS. GEORGE P. *The Medicine Man in Texas,* Houston, 1930. Biographical. OP.

STEPHENS, I. K. *The Hermit Philosopher of Liendo,* Southern Methodist University Press, Dallas, 1951. Well-conceived and well-written biography of Edmund Montgomery — illegitimate son of a Scottish lord, husband of the sculptress Elisabet Ney — who, after being educated in Germany and becoming a member of the Royal College of Physicians of London, came to Texas with his wife and sons and settled on Liendo Plantation, near Hempstead, once known as Sixshooter Junction. Here, in utter isolation from people of cultivated minds, he conducted scientific experiments in his inadequate laboratory and thought out a philosophy said to be half a century ahead of his time. He died in 1911. His life was the drama of an elevated soul of complexities, far more tragic than any life associated with the lurid "killings" around him.

WOODHULL, FROST. "Ranch Remedios," in *Man, Bird, and Beast,* Texas Folklore Society Publication VIII, 1930. The richest and most readable collection of pioneer remedies yet published.

16

Mountain Men

AS USED HERE, the term "Mountain Men" applies to those trappers and traders who went into the Rocky Mountains before emigrants had even sought a pass through them to the west or cattle had beat out a trail on the plains east of them. Beaver fur was the lodestar for the Mountain Men. Their span of activity was brief, their number insignificant. Yet hardly any other distinct class of men, irrespective of number or permanence, has called forth so many excellent books as the Mountain Men. The books are not nearly so numerous as those connected with range life, but when one considers the writings of Stanley Vestal, Sabin, Ruxton, Fergusson, Chittenden, Favour, Garrard, Inman, Irving, Reid, and White in this field, one doubts whether any other form of American life at all has been so well covered in ballad, fiction, biography, history.

See James Hobbs, James O. Pattie, and Reuben Gold Thwaites under "Surge of Life in the West," also "Santa Fe and the Santa Fe Trail."

ALTER, J. CECIL. *James Bridger,* Salt Lake City, 1925. A hogshead of life. Bibliography. OP. Republished by Long's College Book Co., Columbus, Ohio.

BONNER, T. D. *The Life and Adventures of James P. Beckwourth,* 1856; reprinted in 1931, with an illuminating introduction by Bernard DeVoto. OP. Beckwourth was the champion of all western liars.

BREWERTON, G. D. *Overland with Kit Carson,* New York, 1930. Good narrative. OP.

CHITTENDEN, H. M. *The American Fur Trade of the*

Far West, New York, 1902. OP. Basic work. Bibliography.

CLELAND, ROBERT GLASS. *This Reckless Breed of Men: The Trappers and Fur Traders of the Southwest,* Knopf, New York, 1950. Fresh emphasis on the California-Arizona-New Mexico region by a knowing scholar. Economical in style without loss of either humanity or history. Bibliography.

CONRAD, HOWARD L. *Uncle Dick Wootton,* 1890. Primary source. OP.

COYNER, D. H. *The Lost Trappers,* 1847.

DAVIDSON, L. J., and BOSTWICK, P. *The Literature of the Rocky Mountain West 1803-1903,* Caxton, Caldwell, Idaho, 1939. Davidson and Forrester Blake, editors. *Rocky Mountain Tales,* University of Oklahoma Press, Norman, 1947.

DEVOTO, BERNARD. *Across the Wide Missouri,* Houghton Mifflin, Boston, 1947. Superbly illustrated by reproductions of Alfred Jacob Miller. DeVoto has amplitude and is a master of his subject as well as of the craft of writing.

FAVOUR, ALPHEUS H. *Old Bill Williams, Mountain Man,* University of North Carolina Press, Chapel Hill, 1936. Flavor and facts both. Full bibliography.

FERGUSSON, HARVEY. *Rio Grande,* 1933, republished by Tudor, New York. The drama and evolution of human life in New Mexico, written out of knowledge and with power. *Wolf Song,* New York, 1927. OP. Graphic historical novel of Mountain Men. It sings with life.

GARRARD, LEWIS H. *Wah-toyah and the Taos Trail,* 1850. One of the basic works.

GRANT, BLANCHE C. *When Old Trails Were New — The Story of Taos,* New York, 1934. OP. Taos was rendezvous town for the free trappers.

GUTHRIE, A. B., JR. *The Big Sky,* Sloane, New York, 1947 (now published by Houghton Mifflin, Boston). "An unusually original novel, superb as historical fiction." — Bernard DeVoto. I still prefer Harvey Fergusson's *Wolf Song.*

HAMILTON, W. T. *My Sixty Years on the Plains,* New York, 1905. Now published by Long's College Book Co., Columbus, Ohio.

INMAN, HENRY. *The Old Santa Fe Trail*, 1897.

IRVING, WASHINGTON. *The Adventures of Captain Bonneville* and *Astoria*. The latter book was founded on Robert Stuart's Narratives. In 1935 these were prepared for the press, with much illuminative material, by Philip Ashton Rollins and issued under the title of *The Discovery of the Oregon Trail*.

LARPENTEUR, CHARLES. *Forty Years a Fur Trader on the Upper Missouri,* edited by Elliott Coues, New York, 1898. As Milo Milton Quaife shows in an edition of the narrative issued by the Lakeside Press, Chicago, 1933, the indefatigable Coues just about rewrote the old fur trader's narrative. It is immediate and vigorous.

LAUT, A. C. *The Story of the Trapper*, New York, 1902. A popular survey, emphasizing types and characters.

LEONARD, ZENAS. *Narrative of the Adventures of Zenas Leonard,* Clearfield, Pa., 1839. In 1833 the Leonard trappers reached San Francisco Bay, boarded a Boston ship anchored near shore, and for the first time in two years varied their meat diet by eating bread and drinking "Coneac." One of the trappers had a gun named Knock-him-stiff. Such earthy details abound in this narrative of adventures in a brand new world.

LOCKWOOD, FRANK C. *Arizona Characters*, Los Angeles, 1928. Very readable biographic sketches. OP.

MILLER, ALFRED JACOB. *The West of Alfred Jacob Miller,* with an account of the artist by Marvin C. Ross, University of Oklahoma Press, Norman, 1950. Although Miller painted the West during 1837-38, only now is he being discovered by the public. This is mainly a picture book, in the top rank.

PATTIE, JAMES OHIO. *The Personal Narrative of James O. Pattie of Kentucky*, Cincinnati, 1831. Pattie and his small party went west in 1824. For grizzlies, thirst, and other features of primitive adventure the narrative is primary.

REID, MAYNE. *The Scalp Hunters*. An antiquated novel, but it has some deep-dyed pictures of Mountain Men.

Ross, ALEXANDER. *Adventures of the First Settlers on the Oregon or Columbia River* (1849) and *The Fur Hunters of the Far West* (1855). The trappers of the Southwest can no more be divorced from the trappers of the Hudson's Bay Company than can Texas cowboys from those of Montana.

RUSSELL, OSBORNE. *Journal of a Trapper,* Boise, Idaho, 1921. In the winter of 1839, at Fort Hall on Snake River, Russell and three other trappers "had some few books to read, such as Byron, Shakespeare and Scott's works, the Bible and Clark's Commentary on it, and some small works on geology, chemistry and philosophy." Russell was wont to speculate on Life and Nature. In perspective he approaches Ruxton.

RUXTON, GEORGE F. *Life in the Far West,* 1848; reprinted by the University of Oklahoma Press, Norman, 1951, edited by LeRoy R. Hafen. No other contemporary of the Mountain Men has been so much quoted as Ruxton. He remains supremely readable.

SABIN, EDWIN L. *Kit Carson Days,* 1914. A work long standard, rich on rendezvous, bears, and many other associated subjects. Bibliography. Republished in rewritten form, 1935. OP.

VESTAL, STANLEY (pseudonym for Walter S. Campbell). *Kit Carson,* 1928. As a clean-running biographic narrative, it is not likely to be superseded. *Mountain Men,* 1937, OP; *The Old Santa Fe Trail,* 1939. Vestal's "Fandango," a tale of the Mountain Men in Taos, is among the most spirited ballads America has produced. It and a few other Mountain Men ballads are contained in the slight collection, *Fandango,* 1927. Houghton Mifflin, Boston, published the aforementioned titles. *James Bridger, Mountain Man,* Morrow, New York, 1946, is smoother than J. Cecil Alter's biography but not so savory. *Joe Meek, the Merry Mountain Man,* Caxton, Caldwell, Idaho, 1952.

WHITE, STEWART EDWARD. *The Long Rifle,* 1932, and *Ranchero,* 1933, Doubleday, Doran, Garden City, N. Y. Historical fiction.

17

Santa Fe and the Santa Fe Trail

THERE WAS Independence on the Missouri River, then eight hundred miles of twisting trail across hills, plains, and mountains, all uninhabited save by a few wandering Indians and uncountable buffaloes. Then there was Santa Fe. On west of it lay nearly a thousand miles of wild broken lands before one came to the village of Los Angeles. But there was no trail to Los Angeles. At Santa Fe the trail turned south and after crawling over the Jornada del Muerto — Journey of the Dead Man — threading the great Pass of the North (El Paso) and crossing a vast desert, reached Chihuahua City.

Looked at in one way, Santa Fe was a mud village. In another way, it was the solitary oasis of human picturesqueness in a continent of vacancy. Like that of Athens, though of an entirely different quality, its fame was out of all proportion to its size. In a strong chapter, entitled "A Caravan Enters Santa Fe," R. L. Duffus *(The Santa Fe Trail)* elaborates on how for all travelers the town always had "the lure of adventure." Josiah Gregg doubted whether "the first sight of the walls of Jerusalem were beheld with much more tumultuous and soul-enrapturing joy" than Santa Fe was by a caravan topping the last rise and, eight hundred miles of solitude behind it, looking down on the town's shining walls and cottonwoods.

No other town of its size in America has been the subject of and focus for as much good literature as Santa Fe. Pittsburgh and dozens of other big cities all put together have not inspired one tenth of the imaginative play that Santa Fe has inspired. Some of the transcontinental railroads probably carry as much freight in a day as went over the Santa Fe Trail in all the wagons in all the years they pulled over the Santa Fe Trail. But the Santa Fe Trail is one of the three great trails of America that, though plowed under, fenced across, and cemented over, seem destined for perennial travel—by those happily able to go without tourist guides. To quote Robert Louis Stevenson, "The greatest adventures are not those we go to seek." The other two trails comparable to the Santa Fe are also of the West—the Oregon Trail for emigrants and the Chisholm Trail for cattle.

For additional literature see "Mountain Men," "Stagecoaches, Freighting," "Surge of Life in the West."

CATHER, WILLA. *Death Comes for the Archbishop,* Knopf, New York, 1927. Historical novel.

CONNELLEY, W. E. (editor). *Doniphan's Expedition,* 1907. Saga of the Mexican War. OP.

DAVIS, W. W. H. *El Gringo, or New Mexico and Her People,* 1856; reprinted by Rydal, Santa Fe, 1938. OP. Excellent on manners and customs.

DUFFUS, R. L. *The Santa Fe Trail,* New York, 1930. OP. Bibliography. Best book of this century on the subject.

DUNBAR, SEYMOUR. *History of Travel in America,* 1915; revised edition issued by Tudor, New York, 1937.

GREGG, JOSIAH. *Commerce of the Prairies,* two vols., 1844. Reprinted, but all OP. Gregg wrote as a man of experience and not as a professional writer. He wrote not only the classic of the Santa Fe trade and trail but one of the classics of bedrock Americana. It is a commentary on civilization in the Southwest that his work is not kept in print. Harvey Fergusson, in *Rio Grande,* has written a penetrating criticism of the man and his subject. In 1941 and 1944 the University of Oklahoma Press, Norman, issued two volumes of the *Diary and Letters of Josiah Gregg,* edited by Maurice G. Fulton with Introductions by Paul Horgan. These volumes, interesting in themselves, are a valuable complement to Gregg's major work.

INMAN, HENRY. *The Old Santa Fe Trail*, 1897. A mine of lore.

LAUGHLIN, RUTH (formerly Ruth Laughlin Barker). *Caballeros*, New York, 1931; republished by Caxton, Caldwell, Idaho, 1946. Essayical goings into the life of things. Especially delightful on burros. A book to be starred. *The Wind Leaves No Shadow*, New York, 1948; Caxton, 1951. A novel around Doña Tules Barceló, the powerful, beautiful, and silvered mistress of Santa Fe's gambling *sala* in the 1830's and '40's.

MAGOFFIN, SUSAN SHELBY. *Down the Santa Fe Trail*, Yale University Press, New Haven, 1926. Delectable diary.

PILLSBURY, DOROTHY L. *No High Adobe*, University of New Mexico Press, Albuquerque, 1950. Sketches, pleasant to read, that make the *gente* very real.

RUXTON, GEORGE FREDERICK. *Adventures in Mexico and the Rocky Mountains*, London, 1847. In 1924 the second half of this book was reprinted under title of *Wild Life in the Rocky Mountains*. In 1950, with additional Ruxton writings discovered by Clyde and Mae Reed Porter, the book, edited by LeRoy R. Hafen, was reissued under title of *Ruxton of the Rockies*, University of Oklahoma Press, Norman. Santa Fe is only one incident in it. Ruxton illuminates whatever he touches. He was in love with the wilderness and had a fire in his belly. Other writers add details, but Ruxton and Gregg embodied the whole Santa Fe world.

VESTAL, STANLEY. *The Old Santa Fe Trail*, Houghton Mifflin, Boston, 1939.

18

Stagecoaches, Freighting

A GOOD INTRODUCTION to a treatment of the stagecoach of the West would be Thomas De Quincey's "The English Mail-Coach." The proper place to read about the coaches would be in Doctor Lyon's Pony Express Museum, out from Pasadena, California. May it never perish! Old Monte drives up now and then in Alfred Henry Lewis' *Wolfville* tales, and Bret Harte made Yuba Bill crack the whip; but, somehow, considering all the excellent expositions and reminiscing of stage-coaching in western America, the proud, insolent, glorious figure of the driver has not been adequately pictured.

Literature on "Santa Fe and the Santa Fe Trail" is pertinent. See also under "Pony Express."

BANNING, WILLIAM, and BANNING, GEORGE HUGH. *Six Horses*, New York, 1930. A combination of history and autobiography. Routes to and in California; much of Texas. Enjoyable reading. Excellent on drivers, travelers, stations, "pass the mustard, please." Bibliography. OP.

CONKLING, ROSCOE P. and MARGARET B. *The Butterfield Overland Trail, 1857-1869*, Arthur H. Clark Co., Glendale, California. Three volumes replete with facts from politics in Washington over mail contracts to Horsehead Crossing on the Pecos River.

DOBIE, J. FRANK. Chapter entitled "Pistols, Poker and the Petite Mademoiselle in a Stagecoach," in *The Flavor of Texas*, 1936. OP.

DUFFUS, R. L. *The Santa Fe Trail*, New York, 1930. Swift reading. Well selected bibliography. OP.

FREDERICK, J. V. *Ben Holladay, the Stage Coach King,* Clark, Glendale, California, 1940. Bibliography.

HALEY, J. EVETTS. Chapter v, "The Stage-Coach Mail," in *Fort Concho and the Texas Frontier,* illustrated by Harold Bugbee, San Angelo Standard-Times, San Angelo, Texas, 1952. Strong on frontier crossed by stage line.

HUNGERFORD, EDWARD. *Wells Fargo: Advancing the Frontier,* Random House, New York, 1949. Written without regard for the human beings that the all-swallowing corporation crushed. Facts on highwaymen.

INMAN, HENRY. *The Old Santa Fe Trail,* New York, 1897. OP. *The Great Salt Lake Trail,* 1898. OP. Many first-hand incidents and characters.

MAJORS, ALEXANDER. *Seventy Years on the Frontier,* Chicago, 1893. Reprinted by Long's College Book Co., Columbus, Ohio. Majors was the lead steer of all freighters.

ORMSBY, W. L. *The Butterfield Overland Mail,* edited by Lyle H. Wright and Josephine M. Bynum, Huntington Library, San Marino, California, 1942. Ormsby rode the stage from St. Louis to San Francisco in 1858 and contributed to the New York *Herald* the lively articles now made into this book.

ROOT, FRANK A., and CONNELLEY, W. E. *The Overland Stage to California,* Topeka, Kansas, 1901. Reprinted by Long's College Book Co., Columbus, Ohio. A full storehouse. Basic.

SANTLEBEN, AUGUST. *A Texas Pioneer,* edited by I. D. Affleck, New York, 1910. OP. Best treatise available on freighting on Chihuahua Trail.

TWAIN, MARK. *Roughing It,* 1871. Mark Twain went west by stage.

WINTHER, O. O. *Express and Stagecoach Days in California,* Stanford University Press, 1926. Compact, with bibliography. OP.

19

Pony Express

"PRESENTLY the driver exclaims, 'Here he comes!'

"Every neck is stretched and every eye strained. Away across the endless dead level of the prairie a black speck appears against the sky. In a second or two it becomes a horse and rider, rising and falling, rising and falling—sweeping towards us nearer and nearer—growing more and more distinct, more and more sharply defined—nearer and still nearer, and the flutter of the hoofs comes faintly to the ear—another instant a whoop and a hurrah from our upper deck [of the stagecoach], a wave of the rider's hand, but no reply, and man and horse burst past our excited faces, and go swinging away like a belated fragment of a storm."—Mark Twain, *Roughing It.*

A word cannot be defined in its own terms; nor can a region, or a feature of that region. Analogy and perspective are necessary for comprehension. The sense of horseback motion has never been better realized than by Kipling in "The Ballad of East and West." See "Horses."

BRADLEY, GLENN D. *The Story of the Pony Express,* Chicago, 1913. Nothing extra. OP.

BREWERTON, G. D. *Overland with Kit Carson,* New York, 1930. Bibliography on West in general.

CHAPMAN, ARTHUR. *The Pony Express,* Putnam's, New York, 1932. Good reading and bibliography.

DOBIE, J. FRANK. Chapter on "Rides and Riders," in *On the Open Range,* published in 1931; reprinted by Banks Upshaw, Dallas. Chapter on "Under the Saddle" in *The Mustangs*.

HAFEN, LeROY. *The Overland Mail*, Cleveland, 1926. Factual, bibliography. OP.

ROOT, FRANK A., and CONNELLEY, W. E. *The Overland Stage to California*, Topeka, Kansas, 1901. Reprinted by Long's College Book Co., Columbus, Ohio. Basic work.

VISSCHER, FRANK J. *A Thrilling and Truthful History of the Pony Express*, Chicago, 1908. OP. Not excessively "thrilling."

20

Surge of Life in the West

THE WANDERINGS of Cabeza de Vaca, Coronado, De Soto, and La Salle had long been chronicled, although the chronicles had not been popularized in English, when in 1804 Captain Meriwether Lewis and Captain William Clark set out to explore not only the Louisiana Territory, which had just been purchased for the United States by President Thomas Jefferson, but on west to the Pacific. Their *Journals,* published in 1814, initiated a series of chronicles comparable in scope, vitality, and manhood adventure to the great collection known as *Hakluyt's Voyages.*

Between 1904 and 1907 Reuben Gold Thwaites, one of the outstanding editors of the English-speaking world, brought out in thirty-two volumes his epic *Early Western Travels.* This work includes the Lewis and Clark *Journals;* every student of the West, whether Northwest or Southwest, goes to the collection sooner or later. It is a commentary on the values of life held by big rich boasters of patriotism in the West that virtually all the chronicles in the collection remain out of print.

An important addendum to the Thwaites collection of *Early Western Travels* is "The Southwest Historical Series," edited by Ralph P. Bieber — twelve volumes, published 1931-43, by Clark, Glendale, California.

The stampede to California that began in 1849 climaxed all migration orgies of the world in its lust for gold; but the lust for gold was merely one manifestation of a mighty population's lust for life. Railroads raced each other to cross the continent. Ten million Longhorns were going up the trails from Texas while the last of a hundred million buffaloes, killed in herds—the greatest slaughter in history—were being skinned. Dodge City was the Cowboy Capital of the world, and Chicago was becoming "hog butcher of the world." Miller and Lux were expanding their ranges so that, as others boasted, their herds could trail from Oregon to Baja California and bed down every night on Miller and Lux's own grass.

Hubert Howe Bancroft (1832-1918) was massing in San Francisco at his own expense the greatest assemblage of historical documents any one individual ever assembled. While his interviewers and note-takers sorted down tons of manuscript, he was employing a corps of historians to write what, at first designed as a history of the Pacific states, grew in twenty-eight volumes to embrace also Alaska, British Columbia, Texas, Mexico, and Central America, aside from five volumes on the Native Races and six volumes of essays. Meantime he was printing these volumes in sets of thousands and selling them through an army of agents that covered America.

Collis P. Huntington (1821-1900) was building the Southern Pacific Railroad into a network, interlocked with other systems and steamship lines, not only enveloping California land but also the whole economic and political life of that and other states, with headquarters in the U.S. Congress. Then his nephew, Henry E. Huntington (1850-1927), taking over his wealth and power, was building gardens at San Marino, California, collecting art, books, and manuscripts to make, without benefit of any institution of learning and in defiance of all the slow processes of tradition found at Oxford and Harvard, a Huntington Library and a Huntington Art Gallery that, set down amid the most costly botanical profusion imaginable, now rival the world's finest.

The dreams were of empire. Old men and young toiled as "terribly" as mighty Raleigh. The "spacious times" of Queen Elizabeth seemed, indeed, to be translated to another sphere, though here the elements that went into the mixture were less diverse. Boom methods of Gargantuan scale were applied to cultural factors as well as to the physical. Few men stopped to reflect that while objects of art may be bought by the wholesale, the development of genuine culture is too intimately personal and too chemically blended with the spiritual to be bartered for. The Huntingtons paid a quarter of a million dollars for Gainsborough's "The Blue Boy." It is very beautiful. Meanwhile the mustang grapevine waits for some artist to paint the strong and lovely grace of its drapery and thereby to enrich for land-dwellers every valley where it hangs over elm or oak.

Most of the books in this section could be placed in other sections. Many have been. They represent the vigor, vitality, energy, and daring characteristic of our frontiers. To quote Harvey Fergusson's phrase, the adventures of mettle have always had "a tension that would not let them rest."

BARKER, EUGENE C. *The Life of Stephen F. Austin,* Dallas, 1925. Republished by Texas State Historical Association, Austin. Iron-wrought biography of the leader in making Texas Anglo-American.

BELL, HORACE. *Reminiscences of a Ranger, or Early Times in California,* Los Angeles, 1881; reprinted, but OP. In this book and in *On the Old West Coast,* Bell caught the lift and spiritedness of life-hungry men.

BIDWELL, JOHN (1819-1900). *Echoes of the Past,* Chico, California (about 1900). Bidwell got to California several years before gold was discovered. He became foremost citizen and entertained scientists, writers, scholars, and artists at his ranch home. His brief accounts of the trip across the plains and of pioneer society in California are graphic, charming, telling. The book goes in and out of print but is not likely to die.

BILLINGTON, RAY ALLEN. *Westward Expansion: A History of the American Frontier,* Macmillan, New York, 1949. This Alpha to Omega treatise concludes with a seventy-five-page, double-column, fine-print bibliography which not only lists but comments upon most books and articles of any consequence that have been published on frontier history.

BOURKE, JOHN G. *On the Border with Crook*, New York, 1891. Now published by Long's College Book Co., Columbus, Ohio. Bourke had an eager, disciplined mind, at once scientific and humanistic; he had imagination and loyalty to truth and justice; he had a strong body and joyed in frontier exploring. He was a captain in the army but had nothing of the littleness of the army mind exhibited by Generals Nelson Miles and O. O. Howard in their egocentric reminiscences. I rank his book as the meatiest and richest of all books dealing with campaigns against Indians. In its amplitude it includes the whole frontier. General George Crook was a wise, generous, and noble man, but his *Autobiography* (edited by Martin F. Schmitt; University of Oklahoma Press) lacks that power in writing necessary to turn the best subject on earth into a good book and capable also, as Darwin demonstrated, of turning earthworms into a classic.

BURNHAM, FREDERICK RUSSELL. *Scouting on Two Continents*, New York, 1926; reprinted, Los Angeles, 1942. A brave book of enthralling interest. The technique of scouting in the Apache Country is illuminated by that of South Africa in the Boer War. Hunting for life, Major Burnham carried it with him. OP.

DEVOTO, BERNARD. *The Year of Decision 1846*, Houghton Mifflin, Boston, 1943. Critical interpretation as well as depiction. The Mexican War, New Mexico, California, Mountain Men, etc. DeVoto's *Across the Wide Missouri* is wider in spirit, less bound to political complexities. See under "Mountain Men."

EMORY, LIEUTENANT COLONEL WILLIAM H. *Notes of a Military Reconnaissance from Fort Leavenworth, in Missouri, to San Diego, in California, including Part of the Arkansas, Del Norte, and Gila Rivers*, Washington, 1848. Emory's own vivid report is only one item in *Executive Document No. 41*, 30th Congress, 1st Session, with which it is bound. Lieutenant J. W. Albert's *Journal* and additional

Report on New Mexico, St. George Cooke's Odyssey of his march from Santa Fe to San Diego, another *Journal* by Captain A. R. Johnson, the Torrey-Englemann report on botany, illustrated with engravings, all go to make this one of the meatiest of a number of meaty government publications. The Emory part of it has been reprinted by the University of New Mexico Press, under title of *Lieutenant Emory Reports,* Introduction and Notes by Ross Calvin, Albuquerque, 1951.

Emory's great two-volume *Report on United States and Mexican Boundary Survey,* Washington 1857 and 1859, is, aside from descriptions of borderlands and their inhabitants, a veritable encyclopedia, wonderfully illustrated, on western flora and fauna. United States Commissioner on this Boundary Survey (following the Mexican War) was John Russell Bartlett. While exploring from the Gulf of Mexico to the Pacific and far down into Mexico, he wrote *Personal Narrative of Explorations and Incidents in Texas, New Mexico, California, Sonora and Chihuahua,* published in two volumes, New York, 1854. For me very little rewritten history has the freshness and fascination of these strong, firsthand personal narratives, though I recognize many of them as being the stuff of literature rather than literature itself.

FOWLER, JACOB. *The Journal of Jacob Fowler, 1821-1822,* edited by Elliott Coues, New York, 1898. Hardly another chronicle of the West is so Defoe-like in homemade realism, whether on Indians and Indian horses or Negro Paul's experience with the Mexican "Lady" at San Fernando de Taos. Should be reprinted.

GAMBRELL, HERBERT. *Anson Jones: The Last President of Texas,* Garden City, New York, 1948; now distributed by Southern Methodist University Press, Dallas, Texas. Anson Jones was more surged over than surgent. Infused with a larger comprehension than that behind many a world figure, this biography of a provincial figure is perhaps the most artfully written that Texas has produced. It goes into the soul of the man.

HOBBS, JAMES. *Wild Life in the Far West,* Hartford,

1872. Hobbs saw just about all the elephants and heard just about all the owls to be seen and heard in the Far West, including western Mexico. Should be reprinted.

HULBERT, ARCHER BUTLER. *Forty-Niners: The Chronicle of the California Trail*, Little, Brown, Boston, 1931. Hulbert read exhaustively in the exhausting literature by and about the gold hunters rushing to California. Then he wove into a synthetic diary the most interesting and illuminating records on happenings, characters, ambitions, talk, singing, the whole life of the emigrants.

IRVING, WASHINGTON. Irving made his ride into what is now Oklahoma in 1832. He had recently returned from a seventeen-year stay in Europe and was a mature literary man —as mature as a conforming romanticist could become. Prairie life refreshed him. *A Tour on the Prairies*, published in 1835, remains refreshing. It is illuminated by *Washington Irving on the Prairie; or, A Narrative of the Southwest in the Year 1832*, by Henry Leavitt Ellsworth (who accompanied Irving), edited by Stanley T. Williams and Barbara D. Simison, New York, 1937; by *The Western Journals of Washington Irving*, excellently edited by John Francis McDermott, Norman, Oklahoma, 1944; and by Charles J. Latrobe's *The Rambler in North America, 1832-1833*, New York, 1835.

JAMES, MARQUIS. *The Raven*, Bobbs-Merrill, Indianapolis, 1929. Graphic life of Sam Houston.

KURZ, RUDOLPH FRIEDERICH. *Journal of Rudolph Friederich Kurz: . . . His Experiences among Fur Traders and American Indians on the Mississippi and Upper Missouri Rivers, during the Years of 1846-1852*, U.S. Bureau of Ethnology Bulletin 115, Washington, 1937. The public has not had a chance at this book, which was printed rather than published. Kurz both saw and recorded with remarkable vitality. He was an artist and the volume contains many reproductions of his paintings and drawings. One of the most readable and illuminating of western journals.

LEWIS, OSCAR. *The Big Four*, New York, 1938. Railroad magnates.

LOCKWOOD, FRANK C. *Arizona Characters,* Los Angeles, California, 1928. Fresh sketches of representative men. The book deserves to be better known than it is. OP.

LYMAN, GEORGE D. *John Marsh Pioneer,* New York, 1930. Prime biography and prime romance. Laid mostly in California. This book almost heads the list of all biographies of western men. OP.

PARKMAN, FRANCIS. *The Oregon Trail,* 1849. Parkman knew how to write but some other penetrators of the West put down about as much. School assignments have made his book a recognized classic.

PATTIE, JAMES O. *Personal Narrative,* Cincinnati, 1831; reprinted, but OP. Positively gripping chronicle of life in New Mexico and the Californias during Mexican days.

PIKE, ZEBULON M. *The Southwestern Expedition of Zebulon M. Pike,* Philadelphia, 1810. The 1895 edition edited by Elliott Coues is the most useful to students. No edition is in print. Pike's explorations of the Southwest (1806-7) began while the great Lewis and Clark expedition (1804-6) was ending. His journal is nothing like so informative as theirs but is just as readable. *The Lost Pathfinder* is a biography of Pike by W. Eugene Hollon, University of Oklahoma Press, Norman, 1949.

TWAIN, MARK. *Roughing It,* 1872. Mark Twain was a man who wrote and not merely a writer in man-form. He was frontier American in all his fibers. He was drunk with western life at a time when both he and it were standing on tiptoe watching the sun rise over the misty mountain tops, and he wrote of what he had seen and lived before he became too sober. *Roughing It* comes nearer catching the energy, the youthfulness, the blooming optimism, the recklessness, the lust for the illimitable in western life than any other book. It deals largely with mining life, but the surging vitality of this life as reflected by Mark Twain has been the chief common denominator of all American frontiers and was as characteristic of Texas "cattle kings" when grass was free as of Virginia City "nabobs" in bonanza.

21

Range Life: Cowboys, Cattle, Sheep

THE COWBOY ORIGINATED in Texas. The Texas cowboy, along with the Texas cowman, was an evolvement from and a blend of the riding, shooting, frontier-formed southerner, the Mexican-Indian horseback worker with livestock (the vaquero), and the Spanish open-range rancher. The blend was not in blood, but in occupational techniques. I have traced this genesis with more detail in *The Longhorns*. Compared with evolution in species, evolution in human affairs is meteor-swift. The driving of millions of cattle and horses from Texas to stock the whole plains area of North America while, following the Civil War, it was being denuded of buffaloes and secured from Indian domination, enabled the Texas cowboy to set his impress upon the whole ranching industry. The cowboy became the best-known occupational type that America has given the world. He exists still and will long exist, though much changed from the original. His fame derives from the past.

Romance, both genuine and spurious, has obscured the realities of range and trail. The realities themselves have, however, been such that few riders really belonging to the range wished to lead any other existence. Only by force of circumstances have they changed "the grass beneath and the sky above" for a more settled, more confining, and more materially remunerative way of life. Some of the old-time cowboys were little more adaptable to change than the Plains Indians; few were less reluctant to plow or work in houses. Heaven in their dreams was a range better watered than the one they knew, with grass never stricken by drought, plenty of fat cattle, the best horses and comrades of their experience, more of women than they talked about in public, and nothing at all of golden streets, golden harps, angel wings, and thrones; it was a mere extension, somewhat improved, of the present. Bankers, manufacturers, merchants, and mechanics seldom so idealize their own occupations; they work fifty weeks a year to go free the other two.

For every hired man on horseback there have been hundreds of plowmen in America, and tens of millions of acres of rangelands have been plowed under, but who can cite a single autobiography of a laborer in the fields of cotton, of corn, of wheat? Or do coal miners, steelmongers, workers in oil refineries, factory hands of any kind of factory, the employees of chain stores and department stores ever write autobiographies? Many scores of autobiographies have been written by range men, perhaps half of them by cowboys who never became owners at all. A high percentage of the autobiographies are in pamphlet form; many that were written have not been published. The trail drivers of open range days, nearly all dead now, felt the urge to record experiences more strongly than their successors. They realized that they had been a part of an epic life.

The fact that the hired man on horseback has been as good a man as the owner and, on the average, has been a more spirited and eager man than the hand on foot may afford some explanation of the validity and vitality of his chroniclings, no matter how crude they be. On the other hand, the fact that the rich owner and the college-educated aspirant to be a cowboy soon learned, if they stayed on the range, that *a man's a man for a' that* may to some extent account for a certain generous amplitude of character inherent in their most representative reminiscences. Sympathy for the life biases my judgment; that judgment, nevertheless, is that some of the strongest and raciest autobiographic writing produced by America has been by range men.

This is not to say that these chronicles are of a high literary order. Their writers have generally lacked the maturity

Tom Lea, in *The Longhorns* by J. Frank Dobie (1941)

of mind, the reflective wisdom, and the power of observation found in personal narratives of the highest order. No man who camped with a chuck wagon has written anything remotely comparable to Charles M. Doughty's *Arabia Deserta*, a chronicle at once personal and impersonal, restrainedly subjective and widely objective, of his life with nomadic Bedouins. Perspective is a concomitant of civilization. The chronicles of the range that show perspective have come mostly from educated New Englanders, Englishmen, and Scots. The great majority of the chronicles are limited in subject matter to physical activities. They make few concessions to "the desire of the moth for the star"; they hardly enter the complexities of life, including those of sex. In one section of the West at one time the outstanding differences among range men were between owners of sheep and owners of cattle, the ambition of both being to hog the whole country. On another area of the range at another time, the outstanding difference was between little ranchers, many of whom were stealing, and big ranchers, plenty of whom had stolen. Such differences are not exponents of the kind of individualism that burns itself into great human documents.

Seldom deeper than the chronicles does range fiction go below physical surface into reflection, broodings, hungers— the smolderings deep down in a cowman oppressed by drought and mortgage sitting in a rocking chair on a ranch gallery looking at the dust devils and hoping for a cloud; the goings-on inside a silent cowboy riding away alone from an empty pen to which he will never return; the streams of consciousness in a silent man and a silent woman bedded together in a wind-lashed frame house away out on the lone prairie. The wide range of human interests leaves ample room for downright, straightaway narratives of the careers of strong men. If the literature of the range ever matures, however, it will include keener searchings for meanings and harder struggles for human truths by writers who strive in "the craft so long to lerne." For three-quarters of a century the output of fiction on the cowboy has been tremendous, and it shows little diminution. Mass production inundating the masses of readers has made it difficult for serious fictionists writing about range people to get a hearing.

The code of the West was concentrated into the code of the range—and not all of it by any means depended upon the six-shooter. No one can comprehend this code without knowing something about the code of the Old South, whence the Texas cowboy came.

Mexican goats make the best eating in Mexico and mohair has made good money for many ranchers of the Southwest. Goats, goat herders, goatskins, and wine in goatskins figure in the literature of Spain as prominently as six-shooters in Blazing Frontier fiction—and far more pleasantly. Read George Borrow's *The Bible in Spain,* one of the most delectable of travel books. Beyond a few notices of Mexican goat herders, there is on the subject of goats next to nothing readable in American writings. Where there is no competition, supremacy is small distinction; so I should offend no taste by saying that "The Man of Goats" in my own *Tongues of the Monte* is about the best there is so far as goats go.

Although sheep are among the most salient facts of range life, they have, as compared with cattle and horses, been a dim item in the range tradition. Yet, of less than a dozen books on sheep and sheepmen, more than half of them are better written than hundreds of books concerning cowboy life. Mary Austin's *The Flock* is subtle and beautiful; Archer B. Gilfillan's *Sheep* is literature in addition to having much information; Hughie Call's *Golden Fleece* is delightful; Winifred Kupper's *The Golden Hoof* and *Texas Sheepman* have charm—a rare quality in most books on cows and cow people. Among furnishings in the cabin of Robert Maudslay, "the Texas Sheepman," were a set of Sir Walter Scott's works, Shakespeare, and a file of the *Illustrated London News.* "A man who read Shakespeare and the *Illustrated London News* had little to contribute to
> Come a ti yi yoopee
> Ti yi ya!"

O. Henry's ranch experiences in Texas were largely confined to a sheep ranch. The setting of his "Last of the Troubadours" is a sheep ranch. I nominate it as the best range story in American fiction.

"Cowboy Songs" and "Horses" are separate chapters following this. The literature cited in them is mostly range literature, although precious little in all the songs rises to the status of poetry. A considerable part of the literature listed under "Texas Rangers" and "The Bad Man Tradition" bears on range life.

ABBOTT, E. C., and SMITH, HELENA HUNTINGTON. *We Pointed Them North*, New York, 1939. Abbott, better known as Teddy Blue, used to give his address as Three Duce Ranch, Gilt Edge, Montana. Helena Huntington Smith, who actually wrote and arranged his reminiscences, instead of currying him down and putting a checkrein on him, spurred him in the flanks and told him to swaller his head. He did. This book is franker about the women a rollicky cowboy was likely to meet in town than all the other range books put together. The fact that Teddy Blue's wife was a half-breed Indian, daughter of Granville Stuart, and that Indian women do not object to the truth about sex life may account in part for his frankness. The book is mighty good reading. OP.

ADAMS, ANDY. *The Log of a Cowboy* (1903). In 1882, at the age of twenty-three, Andy Adams came to Texas from Indiana. For about ten years he traded horses and drove them up the trail. He knew cattle people and their ranges from Brownsville to Caldwell, Kansas. After mining for another decade, he began to write. If all other books on trail driving were destroyed, a reader could still get a just and authentic conception of trail men, trail work, range cattle, cow horses, and the cow country in general from *The Log of a Cowboy*. It is a novel without a plot, a woman, character development, or sustained dramatic incidents; yet it is the classic of the occupation. It is a simple, straightaway narrative that takes a trail herd from the Rio Grande to the Canadian line, the hands talking as naturally as cows chew cuds, every page illuminated by an easy intimacy with the life. Adams wrote six other books. *The Outlet, A Texas Matchmaker, Cattle Brands,* and *Reed Anthony, Cowman* all make good reading. *Wells Brothers* and *The Ranch on the Beaver* are stories for boys. I read them with pleasure long after I was grown. All but *The Log of a Cowboy* are OP, published by Houghton Mifflin, Boston.

ADAMS, RAMON F. *Cowboy Lingo,* Boston, 1936. A dictionary of cowboy words, figures of speech, picturesque phraseology, slang, etc., with explanations of many factors peculiar to range life. OP. *Western Words,* University of Oklahoma Press, 1944. A companion book. *Come an' Get It,* University of Oklahoma Press, Norman, 1952. Informal exposition of chuck wagon cooks.

ALDRIDGE, REGINALD. *Ranch Notes,* London, 1884. Aldridge, an educated Englishman, got into the cattle business before, in the late eighties, it boomed itself flat. His book is not important, but it is maybe a shade better than *Ranch Life in Southern Kansas and the Indian Territory* by Benjamin S. Miller, New York, 1896. Aldridge and Miller were partners, and each writes kindly about the other.

ALLEN, JOHN HOUGHTON. *Southwest,* Lippincott, Philadelphia, 1952. A chemical compound of highly impressionistic autobiographic nonfiction and highly romantic fiction and folk tales. The setting is a ranch of Mexican tradition in the lower border country of Texas, also saloons and bawdy houses of border towns. Vaqueros and their work in the brush are intensely vivid. The author has a passion for superlatives and for "a joyous cruelty, a good cruelty, a young cruelty."

ARNOLD, OREN, and HALE, J. P. *Hot Irons,* Macmillan, New York, 1940. Technique and lore of cattle brands. OP.

AUSTIN, MARY. *The Flock,* Boston, 1906, OP. Mary Austin saw the meanings of things; she was a creator. Very quietly she sublimated life into the literature of pictures and emotions.

Australian ranching is not foreign to American ranching.

The best book on the subject that I have found is *Pastures New*, by R. V. Billis and A. S. Kenyon, London, 1930.

BARNARD, EVAN G. ("Parson"). *A Rider of the Cherokee Strip*, Houghton Mifflin, Boston, 1936. Savory with little incidents and cowboy humor. OP.

BARNES, WILL C. *Tales from the X-Bar Horse Camp*, Chicago, 1920. OP. Good simple narratives. *Apaches and Longhorns*, Los Angeles, 1941. Autobiography. OP. *Western Grazing Grounds and Forest Ranges*, Chicago, 1913. OP. Governmentally factual. Barnes was in the U.S. Forest Service and was informed.

BARROWS, JOHN R. *Ubet*, Caldwell, Idaho, 1934. Excellent on Northwest; autobiographical. OP.

BECHDOLT, FREDERICK R. *Tales of the Old Timers*, New York, 1924. Vivid, economical stories of "The Warriors of the Pecos" (Billy the Kid and the troubles on John Chisum's ranch-empire), of Butch Cassidy and his Wild Bunch in their Wyoming hide-outs, of the way frontier Texans fought Mexicans and Comanches over the open ranges. Research clogs the style of many historians; perhaps it is just as well that Bechdolt did not search more extensively into the arcana of footnotes. OP.

BOATRIGHT, MODY C. *Tall Tales from Texas Cow Camps*, Dallas, 1934. The tales are tall all right and true to cows that never saw a milk bucket. OP. Reprinted 1946 by Haldeman-Julius, Girard, Kansas.

BOREIN, EDWARD. *Etchings of the West*, edited by Edward S. Spaulding, Santa Barbara, California, 1950. OP. A very handsome folio; primarily a reproduction of sketches, many of which are on range subjects. Ed Borein tells more in them than hundreds of windbags have told in tens of thousands of pages. They are beautiful and authentic, even if they are what post-impressionists call "documentary." Believers in the True Faith say now that Leonardo da Vinci is documentary in his painting of the Lord's Supper. Ed Borein was a great friend of Charlie Russell's but not an imitator. *Etchings of the West* will soon be among the rarities of Western books.

BOWER, B. M. *Chip of the Flying U*, New York, 1904. Charles Russell illustrated this and three other Bower novels. Contrary to his denial, he is supposed to have been the prototype for Chip. A long time ago I read *Chip of the Flying U* and *The Lure of the Dim Trails* and thought them as good as Eugene Manlove Rhodes's stories. That they have faded almost completely out of memory is a commentary on my memory; just the same, a character as well named as Chip should, if he have substance beyond his name, leave an impression even on weak memories. B. M. Bower was a woman, Bower being the name of her first husband. A Montana cowpuncher named "Fiddle Back" Sinclair was her second, and Robert Ellsworth Cowan became the third. Under the name of Bud Cowan he published a book of reminiscences entitled *Range Rider* (Garden City, N. Y., 1930). B. M. Bower wrote a slight introduction to it; neither he nor she says anything about being married to the other. In the best of her fiction she is truer to life than he is in a good part of his nonfiction. Her chaste English is partly explained in an autobiographic note contributed to *Adventure* magazine, December 10, 1924. Her restless father had moved the family from Minnesota to Montana. There, she wrote, he "taught me music and how to draw plans of houses (he was an architect among other things) and to read *Paradise Lost* and Dante and H. Rider Haggard and the Bible and the Constitution—and my taste has been extremely catholic ever since."

BRANCH, E. DOUGLAS. *The Cowboy and His Interpreters*, New York, 1926. Useful bibliography on range matters, and excellent criticism of two kinds of fiction writers. OP.

BRATT, JOHN. *Trails of Yesterday*, Chicago, 1921. John Bratt, twenty-two years old, came to America from England in 1864, went west, and by 1870 was ranching on the Platte. He became a big operator, but his reminiscences, beautifully printed, are stronger on camp cooks and other hired hands than on cattle "kings." Nobody ever heard a cowman call himself or another cowman a king. "Cattle king" is journalese.

BRISBIN, GENERAL JAMES S. *The Beef Bonanza; or, How to Get Rich on the Plains,* Philadelphia, 1881. One of several books of its decade designed to appeal to eastern and European interest in ranching as an investment. Figureless and with more human interest is *Prairie Experiences in Handling Cattle and Sheep,* by Major W. Shepherd (of England), London, 1884.

BRONSON, EDGAR BEECHER. *Cowboy Life on the Western Plains,* Chicago, 1910. *The Red Blooded,* Chicago, 1910. Free-wheeling nonfiction.

BROOKS, BRYANT B. *Memoirs,* Gardendale, California, 1939. The book never was published; it was merely printed to satisfy the senescent vanity of a property-worshiping, cliché-parroting reactionary who made money ranching before he became governor of Wyoming. He tells a few good anecdotes of range days. Numerous better books pertaining to the range are *not* listed here; this mediocrity represents a particular type.

BROTHERS, MARY HUDSON. *A Pecos Pioneer,* University of New Mexico Press, Albuquerque, 1943. Superior to numerous better-known books. See comment under "Women Pioneers."

BROWN, DEE, and SCHMITT, MARTIN F. *Trail Driving Days,* Scribner's, New York, 1952. Primarily a pictorial record, more on the side of action than of realism, except for post-trailing period. Excellent bibliography.

BURTON, HARLEY TRUE. *A History of the J A Ranch,* Austin, 1928. Facts about one of the greatest ranches of Texas and its founder, Charles Goodnight. OP.

CALL, HUGHIE. *Golden Fleece,* Boston, 1942. Hughie married a sheepman, and after mothering the range as well as children with him for a quarter of a century, concluded that Montana is still rather masculine. Especially good on domestic life and on sheepherders. OP.

CANTON, FRANK M. *Frontier Trails,* edited by E. E. Dale, Boston, 1930. OP. Good on tough hombres.

CLAY, JOHN. *My Life on the Range,* privately printed,

Chicago, 1924. OP. John Clay, an educated Scot, came to Canada in 1879 and in time managed some of the largest British-owned ranches of North America. His book is the best of all sources on British-owned ranches. It is just as good on cowboys and sheepherders. Clay was a fine gentleman in addition to being a canny businessman in the realm of cattle and land. He appreciated the beautiful and had a sense of style.

CLELAND, ROBERT GLASS. *The Cattle on a Thousand Hills*, Huntington Library, San Marino, California, 1941 (revised, 1951). Scholarly work on Spanish-Mexican ranching in California.

CLEAVELAND, AGNES MORLEY. *No Life for a Lady*, Houghton Mifflin, Boston, 1941. Best book on range life from a woman's point of view ever published. The setting is New Mexico; humor and humanity prevail.

COLLINGS, ELLSWORTH. *The 101 Ranch*, University of Oklahoma Press, Norman, 1937. The 101 Ranch was far more than a ranch; it was a unique institution. The 101 Ranch Wild West Show is emphasized in this book. OP.

COLLINS, DENNIS. *The Indians' Last Fight or the Dull Knife Raid*, Press of the Appeal to Reason, Girard, Kansas, n.d. Nearly half of this very scarce book deals autobiographically with frontier range life. Realistic, strong, written from the perspective of a man who "wanted something to read" in camp.

COLLINS, HUBERT E. *Warpath and Cattle Trail*, New York, 1928. The pageant of trail life as it passed by a stage stand in Oklahoma; autobiographical. Beautifully printed and illustrated. Far better than numerous other out-of-print books that bring much higher prices in the second-hand market.

CONN, WILLIAM (translator). *Cow-Boys and Colonels: Narrative of a Journey across the Prairie and over the Black Hills of Dakota*, London, 1887; New York (1888?). More of a curiosity than an illuminator, the book is a sparsely annotated translation of *Dans les Montagnes Rocheuses*, by Le Baron E. de Mandat-Grancey, Paris, October, 1884. (The only copy I have examined is of 1889 printing.) It is a gossipy account of an excursion made in 1883-84; cowboys and ranching are viewed pretty much as a sophisticated Parisian views a zoo. The author must have felt more at home with the fantastic Marquis de Mores of Medora, North Dakota. The book appeared at a time when European capital was being invested in western ranches. It was followed by *La Brèche aux Buffles: Un Ranch Français dans le Dakota,* Paris, 1889. Not translated so far as I know.

COOK, JAMES H. *Fifty Years on the Old Frontier,* 1923. Cook came to Texas soon after the close of the Civil War and became a brush popper on the Frio River. Nothing better on cow work in the brush country and trail driving in the seventies has appeared. OP. A good deal of the same material was put into Cook's *Longhorn Cowboy* (Putnam's, 1942), to which the pushing Mr. Howard R. Driggs attached his name.

COOLIDGE, DANE. *Texas Cowboys,* 1937. Thin, but genuine. *Arizona Cowboys,* 1938. *Old California Cowboys,* 1939. All well illustrated by photographs and all OP.

COX, JAMES. *The Cattle Industry of Texas and Adjacent Territory,* St. Louis, 1895. Contains many important biographies and much good history. In 1928 I traded a pair of storebought boots to my uncle Neville Dobie for his copy of this book. A man would have to throw in a young Santa Gertrudis bull now to get a copy.

CRAIG, JOHN R. *Ranching with Lords and Commons,* Toronto, 1903. During the great boom of the early 1880's in the range business, Craig promoted a cattle company in London and then managed a ranch in western Canada. His book is good on mismanaged range business and it is good on people, especially lords, and the land. He attributes to De Quincey a Latin quotation that properly, I think, belongs to Thackeray. He quotes Hamlin Garland: "The trail is poetry; a wagon road is prose; the railroad, arithmetic." He was probably not so good at ranching as at writing. His book supplements *From Home to Home,* by Alex. Staveley Hill, New York, 1885. Hill was a major investor in the Oxley

Ranch, and was, I judge, the pompous cheat and scoundrel that Craig said he was.

CRAWFORD, LEWIS F. *Rekindling Camp Fires: The Exploits of Ben Arnold (Connor)*, Bismarck, North Dakota, 1926. OP. The skill of Lewis F. Crawford of the North Dakota Historical Society made this a richer autobiography than if Arnold had been unaided. He was squaw man, scout, trapper, soldier, deserter, prospector, and actor in other occupations as well as cowboy. He had a fierce sense of justice that extended to Indians. His outlook was wider than that of the average ranch hand. *Badlands and Broncho Trails,* Bismarck, 1922, is a slight book of simple narratives that catches the tune of the Badlands life. OP. *Ranching Days in Dakota,* Wirth Brothers, Baltimore, 1950, is good on horse-raising and the terrible winter of 1886-87.

CULLEY, JOHN. *Cattle, Horses, and Men,* Los Angeles, 1940. Much about the noted Bell Ranch of New Mexico. Especially good on horses. Culley was educated at Oxford. When I visited him in California, he had on his table a presentation copy of a book by Walter Pater. His book has the luminosity that comes from cultivated intelligence. OP.

DACY, GEORGE F. *Four Centuries of Florida Ranching,* St. Louis, 1940. OP. In *Crooked Trails,* Frederic Remington has a chapter (illustrated) on "Cracker Cowboys of Florida," and *Lake Okeechobee,* by A. J. Hanna and Kathryn Abbey, Indianapolis, 1948, treats of modern ranching in Florida, but the range people of that state have been too lethargic-minded to write about themselves and no Marjorie Kinnan Rawlings has settled in their midst to interpret them.

DALE, E. E. *The Range Cattle Industry,* Norman, Oklahoma, 1930. Economic aspects. Bibliography. *Cow Country,* Norman, Oklahoma, 1942. Bully tales and easy history. Both books are OP.

DANA, RICHARD HENRY. *Two Years Before the Mast,* 1841. This transcript of reality has been reprinted many times. It is the classic of the hide and tallow trade of California.

DAVID, ROBERT D. *Malcolm Campbell, Sheriff*, Casper, Wyoming, 1932. Much of the "Johnson County War" between cowmen and thieving nesters. OP.

DAYTON, EDSON C. *Dakota Days*. Privately printed by the author at Clifton Springs, New York, 1937—three hundred copies only. Dayton was more sheepman than cowman. He had a spiritual content. His very use of the word *intellectual* on the second page of his book; his estimate of Milton and Gladstone, adjacent to talk about a frontier saloon; his consciousness of his own inner growth—something no extravert cowboy ever noticed, usually because he did not have it; his quotation to express harmony with nature:

> I have some kinship to the bee,
> I am boon brother with the tree;
> The breathing earth is part of me —

all indicate a refinement that any gambler could safely bet originated in the East and not in Texas or the South.

DOBIE, J. FRANK. *A Vaquero of the Brush Country*, 1929. Much on border troubles over cattle, the "skinning war," running wild cattle in the brush, mustanging, trail driving; John Young's narrative, told in the first person, against range backgrounds. *The Longhorns*, illustrated by Tom Lea, 1941. History of the Longhorn breed, psychology of stampedes; days of maverickers and mavericks; stories of individual lead steers and outlaws of the range; stories about rawhide and many other related subjects. The book attempts to reveal the blend made by man, beast, and range. Both books published by Little, Brown, Boston. *The Mustangs*, 1952. See under "Horses."

FORD, GUS L. *Texas Cattle Brands*, Dallas, 1936. A catalogue of brands. OP.

FRENCH, WILLIAM. *Some Recollections of a Western Ranchman*, London, 1927. A civilized Englishman remembers. OP.

GANN, WALTER. *The Trail Boss*, Boston, 1937. Faithful fiction, with a steer that Charlie Russell should have painted. OP.

GARD, WAYNE. *Frontier Justice,* University of Oklahoma Press, Norman, 1949. This book could be classified under "The Bad Man Tradition," but it has authentic chapters on fence-cutting, the so-called "Johnson County Cattlemen's War" of Wyoming, and other range "difficulties." Clearly written from an equable point of view. Useful bibliography of range books.

GIBSON, J. W. (Watt). *Recollections of a Pioneer,* St. Joseph, Missouri (about 1912). Like many another book concerned only incidentally with range life, this contains essential information on the subject. Here it is trailing cattle from Missouri to California in the 1840's and 1850's. Cattle driving from the East to California was not economically important. The outstanding account on the subject is *A Log of the Texas-California Cattle Trail, 1854,* by James G. Bell, edited

Tom Lea, in *The Longhorns* by J. Frank Dobie (1941)

by J. Evetts Haley, published in the *Southwestern Historical Quarterly*, 1932 (Vols. XXXV and XXXVI). Also reprinted as a separate.

GILFILLAN, ARCHER B. *Sheep*, Boston, 1929. With humor and grace, this sheepherder, who collected books on Samuel Pepys, tells more about sheep dogs, sheep nature, and sheepherder life than any other writer I know. OP.

GIPSON, FRED. *Fabulous Empire*, Houghton Mifflin, Boston, 1946. Biography of Zack Miller of the 101 Ranch and 101 Wild West Show.

GOODWYN, FRANK. *Life on the King Ranch*, Crowell, New York, 1951. The author was reared on the King Ranch. He is especially refreshing on the vaqueros, their techniques and tales.

GRAY, FRANK S. *Pioneer Adventures*, 1948, and *Pioneering in Southwest Texas*, 1949, both printed by the author, Copperas Cove, Texas. These books are listed because the author has the perspective of a civilized gentleman and integrates home life on frontier ranches with range work.

GREER, JAMES K. *Bois d'Arc to Barbed Wire*, Dallas, 1936. Outstanding horse lore. OP.

HAGEDORN, HERMANN. *Roosevelt in the Bad Lands*, Boston, 1921. A better book than Roosevelt's own *Ranch Life and the Hunting Trail*. OP.

HALEY, J. EVETTS. *The XIT Ranch of Texas*, Chicago, 1929. As county and town afford the basis for historical treatment of many areas, ranches have afforded bases for various range country histories. Of such this is tops. A lawsuit for libel brought by one or more individuals mentioned in the book put a stop to the selling of copies by the publishers and made it very "rare." *Charles Goodnight, Cowman and Plainsman*, Boston, 1936, reissued by University of Oklahoma Press, Norman, 1949. Goodnight, powerful individual and extraordinary observer, summed up in himself the whole life of range and trail. Haley's book, packed with realities of incident and character, paints him against a mighty background. *George W. Littlefield, Texan*, University of Oklahoma Press,

Norman, Okla., 1943, is a lesser biography of a lesser man.

HAMILTON, W. H. *Autobiography of a Cowman*, in *South Dakota Historical Collections*, XIX (1938), 475-637. A first-rate narrative of life on the Dakota range.

HAMNER, LAURA V. *Short Grass and Longhorns*, Norman, Oklahoma, 1943. Sketches of Panhandle ranches and ranch people. OP.

HARRIS, FRANK. *My Reminiscences as a Cowboy*, 1930. A blatant farrago of lies, included in this list because of its supreme worthlessness. However, some judges might regard the debilitated and puerile lying in *The Autobiography of Frank Tarbeaux*, as told to Donald H. Clarke, New York, 1930, as equally worthless.

HART, JOHN A., and Others. *History of Pioneer Days in Texas and Oklahoma*. No date or place of publication; no table of contents. This slight book was enlarged into *Pioneer Days in the Southwest from 1850 to 1879*, "Contributions by Charles Goodnight, Emanuel Dubbs, John A. Hart and Others," Guthrie, Oklahoma, 1909. Good on the way frontier ranch families lived. The writers show no sense of humor and no idea of being literary.

HASTINGS, FRANK S. *A Ranchman's Recollections*, Chicago, 1921. OP. Hastings was urbane, which means he had perspective; "Old Gran'pa" is the most pulling cowhorse story I know.

HENRY, O. *Heart of the West*. Interpretative stories of Texas range life, which O. Henry for a time lived. His range stories are scattered through several volumes. "The Last of the Troubadours" is a classic.

HENRY, STUART. *Our Great American Plains*, New York, 1930. OP. An unworshipful, anti-Philistinic picture of Abilene, Kansas, when it was at the end of the Chisholm Trail. While not a primary range book, this is absolutely unique in its analysis of cow-town society, both citizens and drovers. Stuart Henry came to Abilene as a boy in 1868. His brother was the first mayor of the town. After graduating from the University of Kansas in 1881, he in time acquired "the habit of authorship." He had written a book on London and *French Essays and Profiles* and *Hours with Famous Parisians* before he returned to Kansas for a subject. Some of his non-complimentary characterizations of westerners aroused a mighty roar among panegyrists of the West. They did not try to refute his anecdote about the sign of the Bull Head Saloon. This sign showed the whole of a great red bull. The citizens of Abilene were used to seeing bulls driven through town and they could go out any day and see bulls with cows on the prairie. Nature might be good, but any art suggesting nature's virility was indecent. There was such an uprising of Victorian taste that what distinguishes a bull from a cow had to be painted out. A similar artistic operation had to be performed on the bull signifying Bull Durham tobacco—once the range favorite for making cigarettes.

HILL, J. L. *The End of the Cattle Trail*, Long Beach, California [May, 1924]. Rare and meaty pamphlet.

HOLDEN, W. C. *Rollie Burns*, Dallas, 1932. Biography of a Plains cowman. OP. *The Spur Ranch*, Boston, 1934. History of a great Texas ranch. OP.

HORN, TOM. *Life of Tom Horn ... Written by Himself, together with His Letters and Statements by His Friends, A Vindication*. Published (for John C. Coble) by the Louthan Book Company, Denver, 1904. Who wrote the book has been somewhat in debate. John C. Coble's name is signed to the preface attributing full authorship to Horn. Of Pennsylvania background, wealthy and educated, he had employed Horn as a stock detective on his Wyoming ranch. He had the means and ability to see the book through the press. A letter from his wife to me, from Cheyenne, June 21, 1926, says that Horn wrote the book. Charles H. Coe, who succeeded Horn as stock detective in Wyoming, says in *Juggling a Rope* (Pendleton, Oregon, 1927, p. 108), that Horn wrote it. I have a copy, bought from Fred Rosenstock of the Bargain Book Store in Denver, who got it from Hattie Horner Louthan, of Denver also. For years she taught English in the University of Denver, College of Commerce, and is the author of more than one textbook. The Louthan Book Company of Denver was owned by her family. This copy of *Tom Horn* contains her bookplate. On top of the first page of the preface is written in pencil: "I wrote this — 'Ghost wrote.' H. H. L." Then, penciled at the top of the first page of "Closing Word," is "I wrote this."

Glendolene Myrtle Kimmell was a schoolteacher in the country where Tom Horn operated. As her picture shows, she was lush and beautiful. Pages 287-309 print "Miss Kimmell's Statement." She did her best to keep Tom Horn from hanging. She frankly admired him and, it seems to me, loved him. Jay Monaghan, *The Legend of Tom Horn, Last of the Bad Men,* Indianapolis and New York, 1946, says (p. 267), without discussion or proof, that after Horn was hanged and buried Miss Kimmell was "writing a long manuscript about a Sir Galahad horseman who was 'crushed between the grinding stones of two civilizations,' but she never found a publisher who thought her book would sell. It was entitled *The True Life of Tom Horn.*"

The main debate has been over Horn himself. The books about him are not highly important, but they contribute to a spectacular and highly controversial phase of range history, the so-called Johnson County War of Wyoming. Mercer's *Banditti of the Plains,* Mokler's *History of Natrona County, Wyoming,* Canton's *Frontier Trails,* and David's *Malcolm Campbell, Sheriff* (all listed in this chapter) are primary sources on the subject.

HOUGH, EMERSON. *The Story of the Cowboy,* New York, 1897. Exposition not nearly so good as Philip Ashton Rollins' *The Cowboy. North of 36,* New York, 1923. Historical novel of the Chisholm Trail. The best character in it is Old Alamo, lead steer. A young woman owner of the herd trails with it. The success of the romance caused Emerson Hough to advise his friend Andy Adams to put a woman in a novel about trail driving—so Andy Adams told me. Adams replied that a woman with a trail herd would be as useless as a fifth wheel on a wagon and that he would not violate reality by having her. For a devastation of Hough's use of history in *North of 36* see the Appendix in Stuart Henry's *Conquering Our Great American Plains.* Yet the novel does have the right temper.

HOYT, HENRY F. *A Frontier Doctor,* Boston, 1929. Texas Panhandle and New Mexico during Billy the Kid days. Reminiscences.

HUNT, FRAZIER. *Cap Mossman: Last of the Great Cowmen,* illustrated by Ross Santee, Hastings House, New York, 1951. Few full-length biographies of big operators among cowmen have been written. This reveals not only Cap Mossman's operations on enormous ranges, but the man.

HUNTER, J. MARVIN (compiler). *The Trail Drivers of Texas,* two volumes, Bandera, Texas, 1920, 1923. Reprinted in one volume, 1925. All OP. George W. Saunders, founder of the Old Time Trail Drivers Association and for many years president, prevailed on hundreds of old-time range and trail men to write autobiographic sketches. He used to refer to Volume II as the "second edition"; just the same, he was not ignorant, and he had a passion for the history of his people. The chronicles, though chaotic in arrangement, comprise basic source material. An index to the one-volume edition of *The Trail Drivers of Texas* is printed as an appendix to *The Chisholm Trail and Other Routes,* by T. U. Taylor, San Antonio, 1936—a hodgepodge.

JAMES, WILL. *Cowboys North and South,* New York, 1924. *The Drifting Cowboy,* 1925. *Smoky*—a cowhorse story —1930. Several other books, mostly repetitious. Will James knew his frijoles, but burned them up before he died, in 1942. He illustrated all his books. The best one is his first, written before he became sophisticated with life—without becoming in the right way more sophisticated in the arts of drawing and writing. *Lone Cowboy: My Life Story* (1930) is without a date or a geographical location less generalized than the space between Canada and Mexico.

JAMES, W. S. *Cowboy Life in Texas,* Chicago, 1893. A genuine cowboy who became a genuine preacher and wrote a book of validity. This is the best of several books of reminiscences by cowboy preachers, some of whom are as lacking in the real thing as certain cowboy artists. Next to *Cowboy Life in Texas,* in its genre, might come *From the Plains to the Pulpit,* by J. W. Anderson, Houston, 1907. The second edition (reset) has six added chapters. The third, and final, edition, Goose Creek, Texas, 1922, again reset, has another added chapter. J. B. Cranfill was a trail driver from a rough range before he became a Baptist preacher and publisher. His bulky *Chronicle, A Story of Life in Texas,* 1916, is downright and concrete.

KELEHER, WILLIAM A. *Maxwell Land Grant: A New Mexico Item,* Santa Fe, 1942. The Maxwell grant of 1,714,764 acres on the Cimarron River was at one time perhaps the most famous tract of land in the West. This history brings in ranching only incidentally; it focuses on the land business, including grabs by Catron, Dorsey, and other affluent politicians. Perhaps stronger on characters involved during long litigation over the land, and containing more documentary evidence, is *The Grant That Maxwell Bought,* by F. Stanley, The World Press, Denver, 1952 (a folio of 256 pages in an edition of 250 copies at $15.00). Keleher is a lawyer; Stanley is a priest. Harvey Fergusson in his historical novel *Grant of Kingdom,* New York, 1950, vividly supplements both. Keleher's second book, *The Fabulous Frontier,* Rydal, Santa Fe, 1945, illuminates connections between ranch lands and politicians; principally it sketches the careers of A. B. Fall, John Chisum, Pat Garrett, Oliver Lee, Jack Thorp, Gene Rhodes, and other New Mexico notables.

KENT, WILLIAM. *Reminiscences of Outdoor Life,* San Francisco, 1929. OP. This is far from being a straight-out range book. It is the easy talk of an urbane man associated with ranches and ranch people who was equally at home in a Chicago office and among fellow congressmen. He had a country-going nature and gusto for character.

KING, FRANK M. *Wranglin' the Past,* Los Angeles, 1935. King went all the way from Texas to California, listening and looking. OP. His second book, *Longhorn Trail Drivers* (1940), is worthless. His *Pioneer Western Empire Builders* (1946) and *Mavericks* (1947) are no better. Most of the contents of these books appeared in *Western Livestock Journal*, Los Angeles.

KUPPER, WINIFRED. *The Golden Hoof*, New York, 1945. Story of the sheep and sheep people of the Southwest. Facts, but, above that, truth that comes only through imagination and sympathy. OP. *Texas Sheepman*, University of Texas Press, Austin, 1951. The edited reminiscences of Robert Maudslay. He drove sheep all over the West, and lived up to the ideals of an honest Englishman in writing as well as in ranching. He had a sense of humor.

LAMPMAN, CLINTON PARKS. *The Great Western Trail*, New York, 1939. OP. In the upper bracket of autobiographic chronicles, by a sensitive man who never had the provincial point of view. Lampman contemplated as well as observed. He felt the pathos of human destiny.

LANG, LINCOLN A. *Ranching with Roosevelt*, Philadelphia, 1926. Civilized. OP.

LEWIS, ALFRED HENRY. *Wolfville* (1897) and other Wolfville books. All OP. Sketches and rambling stories faithful to cattle backgrounds; flavor and humanity through fictionized anecdote. "The Old Cattleman," who tells all the Wolfville stories, is a substantial and flavorsome creation.

LOCKWOOD, FRANK C. *Arizona Characters*, Los Angeles, 1928. Skilfully written biographies. OP.

McCARTY, JOHN L. *Maverick Town*, University of Oklahoma Press, 1946. Tascosa, Texas, on the Canadian River, with emphasis on the guns.

McCAULEY, JAMES EMMIT. *A Stove-up Cowboy's Story*, with Introduction by John A. Lomax and Illustrations by Tom Lea, Austin, 1943. OP. "My parents be poor like Job's turkey," McCauley wrote. He was a common cowhand with uncommon saltiness of speech. He wrote as he talked. "God pity the wight for whom this vivid, honest story has no interest," John Lomax pronounced. It is one of several brief books of reminiscences brought out in small editions in the "Range Life Series," under the editorship of J. Frank Dobie, by the Texas Folklore Society. The two others worth having are *A Tenderfoot Kid on Gyp Water*, by Carl Peters Benedict (1943) and *Ed Nichols Rode a Horse*, as told to Ruby Nichols Cutbirth (1943).

McCoy, Joseph G. *Historic Sketches of the Cattle Trade of the West and Southwest*, Kansas City, 1874. In 1867, McCoy established at Abilene, Kansas, terminus of the Chisholm Trail, the first market upon which Texas drovers could depend. He went broke and thereupon put his sense, information, and vinegar into the first of all range histories. It is a landmark. Of the several reprinted editions, the one preferred is that edited by Ralph P. Bieber, with an information-packed introduction and many illuminating notes, Glendale, California, 1940. This is Volume VIII in the "Southwest Historical Series," edited by Bieber, and the index to it is included in the general index to the whole series. Available is an edition published by Long's College Book Co., Columbus, Ohio. About the best of original sources on McCoy is *Twenty Years of Kansas City's Live Stock and Traders*, by Cuthbert Powell, Kansas City, 1893 — one of the rarities.

Mackay, Malcolm S. *Cow Range and Hunting Trail*, New York, 1925. Among the best of civilized range books. Fresh observations and something besides ordinary narrative. OP. Illustrations by Russell.

Mandat-Grancey, Baron E. de. See Conn, William.

Mercer, A. S. *Banditti of the Plains, or The Cattlemen's Invasion of Wyoming in 1892*, Cheyenne, 1894; reprinted at Chicago in 1923 under title of *Powder River Invasion, War on the Rustlers in 1892*, "Rewritten by John Mercer Boots." Reprinted 1935, with Foreword by James Mitchell Clarke, by the Grabhorn Press, San Francisco. All editions OP. Bloody troubles between cowmen and nesters in Wyoming, the "Johnson County War." For more literature on the subject, consult the entry under Tom Horn in this chapter.

MILLER, LEWIS B. *Saddles and Lariats,* Boston, 1912. A fictional chronicle, based almost entirely on facts, of a trail herd that tried to get to California in the fifties. The author was a Texan. OP.

MOKLER, ALFRED JAMES. *History of Natrona County, Wyoming, 1888-1922,* Chicago, 1923. Contains some good material on the "Johnson County War." This book is listed as an illustration of many county histories of western states containing concrete information on ranching. Other examples of such county histories are S. D. Butcher's *Pioneer History of Custer County* (Nebraska), Broken Bow, Nebraska, 1901; *History of Jack County* (Texas), Jacksboro, Texas (about 1935); *Historical Sketch of Parker County and Weatherford, Texas,* St. Louis, 1877.

MORA, JO. *Trail Dust and Saddle Leather,* Scribner's, New York, 1946. No better exposition anywhere, and here tellingly illustrated, of reatas, spurs, bits, saddles, and other gear. *Californios,* Doubleday, Garden City, N. Y., 1949. Profusely illustrated. Largely on vaquero techniques. Jo Mora knew the California vaquero, but did not know the range history of other regions and, therefore, judged as unique what was widespread.

NIMMO, JOSEPH, JR. *The Range and Ranch Cattle Traffic in the Western States and Territories,* Executive Document No. 267, House of Representatives, 48th Congress, 2nd Session, Washington, D. C., 1885. Printed also in one or more other government documents. A statistical record concerning grazing lands, trail driving, railroad shipping of cattle, markets, foreign investments in ranches, etc. This document is the outstanding example of factual material to be found in various government publications, Volume III of the *Tenth Census of the United States* (1880) being another. *The Western Range: Letter from the Secretary of Agriculture,* etc. (a "letter" 620 pages long), United States Government Printing Office, Washington, 1936, lists many government publications both state and national.

NORDYKE, LEWIS. *Cattle Empire,* Morrow, New York, 1949. History, largely political, of the XIT Ranch. Not so careful in documentation as Haley's *XIT Ranch of Texas,* and not so detailed on ranch operations, but thoroughly illuminative on the not-heroic side of big businessmen in big land deals. The two histories complement each other.

O'NEIL, JAMES B. *They Die But Once,* New York, 1935. The biographical narrative of a Tejano who vigorously swings a very big loop; fine illustration of the fact that a man can lie authentically. OP.

OSGOOD, E. S. *The Day of the Cattleman,* Minneapolis, 1929. Excellent history and excellent bibliography. Northwest. OP.

PEAKE, ORA BROOKS. *The Colorado Range Cattle Industry,* Clark, Glendale, California, 1937. Dry on facts, but sound in scholarship. Bibliography.

PELZER, LOUIS. *The Cattlemen's Frontier,* Clark, Glendale, California, 1936. Economic treatment, faithful but static. Bibliography.

PENDER, ROSE. *A Lady's Experiences in the Wild West in 1883,* London (1883?); second printing with a new preface, 1888. Rose Pender and two fellow-Englishmen went through Wyoming ranch country, stopping on ranches, and she, a very intelligent, spirited woman, saw realities that few other chroniclers suggest. This is a valuable bit of social history.

PERKINS, CHARLES E. *The Pinto Horse,* Santa Barbara, California, 1927. *The Phantom Bull,* Boston, 1932. Fictional narratives of veracity; literature. OP.

PILGRIM, THOMAS (under pseudonym of Arthur Morecamp). *Live Boys; or Charley and Nasho in Texas,* Boston, 1878. The chronicle, little fictionized, of a trail drive to Kansas. So far as I know, this is the first narrative printed on cattle trailing or cowboy life that is to be accounted authentic. The book is dated from Kerrville, Texas.

PONTING, TOM CANDY. *The Life of Tom Candy Ponting,* Decatur, Illinois [1907], reprinted, with Notes and Introduction by Herbert O. Brayer, by Branding Iron Press,

Evanston, Illinois, 1952. An account of buying cattle in Texas in 1853, driving them to Illinois, and later shipping some to New York. Accounts of trail driving before about 1870 have been few and obscurely printed. The stark diary kept by George C. Duffield of a drive from San Saba County, Texas, to southern Iowa in 1866 is as realistic—often agonizing—as anything extant on this much romanticized subject. It is published in *Annals of Iowa*, Des Moines, IV (April, 1924), 243-62.

POTTER, JACK. Born in 1864, son of the noted "fighting parson," Andrew Jackson Potter, Jack became a far-known trail boss and ranch manager. His first published piece, "Coming Down the Trail," appeared in *The Trail Drivers of Texas*, compiled by J. Marvin Hunter, and is about the livest thing in that monumental collection. Jack Potter wrote for various Western magazines and newspapers. He was more interested in cow nature than in gun fights; he had humor and imagination as well as mastery of facts and a tangy language, though small command over form. His privately printed booklets are: *Lead Steer* (with Introduction by J. Frank Dobie), Clayton, N. M., 1939; *Cattle Trails of the Old West* (with map), Clayton, N.M., 1935; *Cattle Trails of the Old West* (virtually a new booklet), Clayton, N. M., 1939. All OP.

Prose and Poetry of the Live Stock Industry of the United States, Denver, 1905. Biographies of big cowmen and history based on genuine research. The richest in matter of all the hundred-dollar-and-up rare books in its field.

RAINE, WILLIAM McLEOD, and BARNES, WILL C. *Cattle*, Garden City, N. Y., 1930. A succinct and vivid focusing of much scattered history. OP.

RAK, MARY KIDDER. *A Cowman's Wife*, Houghton Mifflin, Boston, 1934. Unglossed, impersonal realism about life on a small modern Arizona ranch. *Mountain Cattle*, 1936, and OP, is an extension of the first book.

REMINGTON, FREDERIC. *Pony Tracks*, New York, 1895 (now published by Long's College Book Co., Columbus,

Ohio); *Crooked Trails*, New York, 1898. Sketches and pictures.

RHODES, EUGENE MANLOVE. *West Is West, Once in the Saddle, Good Men and True, Stepsons of Light,* and other novels. "Gene" Rhodes had the "right tune." He achieved a style that can be called literary. *The Hired Man on Horseback,* by May D. Rhodes, is a biography of the writer. Perhaps "Pasó Por Aquí" will endure as his masterpiece. Rhodes had an intense loyalty to his land and people; he was as gay, gallant, and witty as he was earnest. More than most Western writers, Rhodes was conscious of art. He had the common touch and also he was a writer for writing men. The elements of simplicity and the right kind of sophistication, always with generosity and with an unflagging zeal for the rights of human beings, were mixed in him. The reach of any ample-natured man exceeds his grasp. Rhodes was ample-natured, but he cannot be classed as great because his grasp was too often disproportionately short of the long reach. His fiction becomes increasingly dated.

The Best Novels and Stories of Eugene Manlove Rhodes, edited by Frank V. Dearing, Houghton Mifflin, Boston, 1949, contains an introduction, with plenty of anecdotes and too much enthusiasm, by J. Frank Dobie.

RICHARDS, CLARICE E. *A Tenderfoot Bride,* Garden City, N. Y., 1920. The experiences of a ranchman's wife in Colorado. The telling has charm, warmth, and flexibility. In the way that art is always truer than a literal report, *A Tenderfoot Bride* brings out truths of life that the literalistic *A Cowman's Wife* by Mary Kidder Rak misses.

RICHTER, CONRAD. *The Sea of Grass,* Knopf, New York, 1937. A poetic portrait in fiction, with psychological values, of a big cowman and his wife.

RICKETTS, W. P. *50 Years in the Saddle,* Sheridan, Wyoming, 1942. OP. A natural book with much interesting information. It contains the best account of trailing cattle from Oregon to Wyoming that I have seen.

RIDINGS, SAM P. *The Chisholm Trail*, 1926. Sam P. Ridings, a lawyer, published this book himself from Medford, Oklahoma. He had gone over the land, lived with range men, studied history. A noble book, rich in anecdote and character. The subtitle reads: "A History of the World's Greatest Cattle Trail, together with a Description of the Persons, a Narrative of the Events, and Reminiscences associated with the Same." OP.

ROBINSON, FRANK C. *A Ram in a Thicket*, Abelard Press, New York, 1950. Robinson is the author of many Westerns, none of which I have read. This is an autobiography, here noted because it reveals a maturity of mind and an awareness of political economy and social evolution hardly suggested by other writers of Western fiction.

ROLLINS, ALICE WELLINGTON. *The Story of a Ranch*, New York, 1885. Philip Ashton Rollins (no relation that I know of to Alice Wellington Rollins) went into Charlie Everitt's bookstore in New York one day and said, "I want every book with the word *cowboy* printed in it." *The Story of a Ranch* is listed here to illustrate how titles often have nothing to do with subject. It is without either story or ranch; it is about some dilettanteish people who go out to a Kansas sheep farm, talk Chopin, and wash their fingers in finger bowls.

ROLLINS, PHILIP ASHTON. *The Cowboy*, Scribner's, New York, 1924. Revised, 1936. A scientific exposition; full. Rollins wrote two Western novels, not important. A wealthy man with ranch experience, he collected one of the finest libraries of Western books ever assembled by any individual and presented it to Princeton University.

ROLLINSON, JOHN K. *Pony Trails in Wyoming*, Caldwell, Idaho, 1941. Not inspired and not indispensable, but honest autobiography. OP. *Wyoming Cattle Trails*, Caxton, Caldwell, Idaho, 1948. A more significant book than the autobiography. Good on trailing cattle from Oregon.

ROOSEVELT, THEODORE. *Ranch Life and the Hunting Trail*, New York, 1888. Roosevelt understood the West. He became the peg upon which several range books were hung, Hagedorn's *Roosevelt in the Bad Lands* and Lang's *Ranching with Roosevelt* in particular. A good summing up, with bibliography, is *Roosevelt and the Stockman's Association*, by Ray H. Mattison, pamphlet issued by the State Historical Society of North Dakota, Bismarck, 1950.

RUSH, OSCAR. *The Open Range,* Salt Lake City, 1930. Reprinted 1936 by Caxton, Caldwell, Idaho. A sensitive range man's response to natural things. The subtitle, *Bunk House Philosophy,* characterizes the book.

RUSSELL, CHARLES M. *Trails Plowed Under,* 1927, with introduction by Will Rogers. Russell was the greatest painter that ever painted a range man, a range cow, a range horse or a Plains Indian. He savvied the cow, the grass, the blizzard, the drought, the wolf, the young puncher in love with his own shadow, the old waddie remembering rides and thirsts of far away and long ago. He was a wonderful storyteller, and most of his pictures tell stories. He never generalized, painting "a man," "a horse," "a buffalo" in the abstract. His subjects are warm with life, whether awake or asleep, at a particular instant, under particular conditions. *Trails Plowed Under,* prodigally illustrated, is a collection of yarns and anecdotes saturated with humor and humanity. It incorporates the materials in two Rawhide Rawlins pamphlets. *Good Medicine,* published posthumously, is a collection of Russell's letters, illustrations saying more than written words.

Russell's illustrations have enriched numerous range books, B. M. Bower's novels, Malcolm S. Mackay's *Cow Range and Hunting Trail,* and Patrick T. Tucker's *Riding the High Country* being outstanding among them. Tucker's book, autobiography, has a bully chapter on Charlie Russell. *Charles M. Russell, the Cowboy Artist: A Bibliography,* by Karl Yost, Pasadena, California, 1948, is better composed than its companion biography, *Charles M. Russell the Cowboy Artist,* by Ramon F. Adams and Homer E. Britzman. (Both OP.) One of the most concrete pieces of writing on Russell is a chapter in *In the Land of Chinook,* by Al. J.

Noyes, Helena, Montana, 1917. "Memories of Charlie Russell," in *Memories of Old Montana,* by Con Price, Hollywood, 1945, is also good. All right as far as it goes, about a rock's throw away, is "The Conservatism of Charles M. Russell," by J. Frank Dobie, in a portfolio reproduction of *Seven Drawings by Charles M. Russell, with an Additional Drawing by Tom Lea,* printed by Carl Hertzog, El Paso [1950].

SANTEE, ROSS. *Cowboy,* 1928. OP. The plotless narrative, reading like autobiography, of a kid who ran away from a farm in East Texas to be a cowboy in Arizona. His cowpuncher teachers are the kind "who know what a cow is thinking of before she knows herself." Passages in *Cowboy* combine reality and elemental melody in a way that almost no other range writer excepting Charles M. Russell has achieved. Santee is a pen-and-ink artist also. Among his other books, *Men and Horses* is about the best.

SHAW, JAMES C. *North from Texas: Incidents in the Early Life of a Range Man in Texas, Dakota and Wyoming, 1852-1883,* edited by Herbert O. Brayer. Branding Iron Press, Evanston, Illinois, 1952. Edition limited to 750 copies. I first met this honest autobiography by long quotations from it in Virginia Cole Trenholm's *Footprints on the Frontier* (Douglas, Wyoming, 1945), wherein I learned that Shaw's narrative had been privately printed in Cheyenne in 1931, in pamphlet form, for gifts to a few friends and members of the author's family. I tried to buy a copy but could find none for sale at any price. This reprint is in a format suitable to the economical prose, replete with telling incidents and homely details. It will soon be only a little less scarce than the original.

SHEEDY, DENNIS. *The Autobiography of Dennis Sheedy.* Privately printed in Denver, 1922 or 1923. Sixty pages bound in leather and as scarce as psalm-singing in "fancy houses." The item is not very important in the realm of range literature but it exemplifies the successful businessman that the judicious cowman of open range days frequently became.

SHEFFY, L. F. *The Life and Times of Timothy Dwight Hobart, 1855-1935*, Panhandle-Plains Historical Society, Canyon, Texas, 1950. Hobart was manager for the large J A Ranch, established by Charles Goodnight. He had a sense of history. This mature biography treats of important developments pertaining to ranching in the Texas Panhandle.

SIRINGO, CHARLES A. *A Texas Cowboy, or Fifteen Years on the Hurricane Deck of a Spanish Cow Pony*, 1885. The first in time of all cowboy autobiographies and first, also, in plain rollickiness. Siringo later told the same story with additions under the titles of *A Lone Star Cowboy, A Cowboy Detective*, etc., all out of print. Finally, there appeared his *Riata and Spurs*, Boston, 1927, a summation and extension of previous autobiographies. Because of a threatened lawsuit, half of it had to be cut and additional material provided for a "Revised Edition." No other cowboy ever talked about himself so much in print; few had more to talk about. I have said my full say on him in an introduction, which includes a bibliography, to *A Texas Cowboy*, published with Tom Lea illustrations by Sloane, New York, 1950. OP.

SMITH, ERWIN E., and HALEY, J. EVETTS. *Life on the Texas Range*, photographs by Smith and text by Haley, University of Texas Press, Austin, 1952. Erwin Smith yearned and studied to be a sculptor. Early in this century he went with camera to photograph the life of land, cattle, horses, and men on the big ranches of West Texas. In him feeling and perspective of artist were fused with technical mastership. "I don't mean," wrote Tom Lea, "that he made just the best photographs I ever saw on the subject. I mean the best pictures. That includes paintings, drawings, prints." On 9 by 12 pages of 100-pound antique finish paper, the photographs are superbly reproduced. Evetts Haley's introduction interprets as well as chronicles the life of a strange and tragic man. The book is easily the finest range book in the realm of the pictorial ever published.

SMITH, WALLACE. *Garden of the Sun,* Los Angeles, 1939. OP. Despite the banal title, this is a scholarly work with first-rate chapters on California horses and ranching in the San Joaquin Valley.

SNYDER, A. B., as told to Nellie Snyder Yost. *Pinnacle Jake,* Caxton, Caldwell, Idaho, 1951. The setting is Nebraska, Wyoming, and Montana from the 1880's on. Had Pinnacle Jake kept a diary, his accounts of range characters, especially camp cooks and range horses, with emphasis on night horses and outlaws, could not have been fresher or more precise in detail. Reading this book will not give a new interpretation of open range work with big outfits, but the aliveness of it in both narrative and sketch makes it among the best of old-time cowboy reminiscences.

SONNICHSEN, C. L. *Cowboys and Cattle Kings: Life on the Range Today,* University of Oklahoma Press, Norman, 1950. An interviewer's findings without the historical criticism exemplified by Bernard DeVoto on the subject of federal-owned ranges (in essays in *Harper's Magazine* during the late 1940's).

STANLEY, CLARK, "better known as the Rattlesnake King." *The Life and Adventures of the American Cow-Boy,* published by the author at Providence, Rhode Island, 1897. This pamphlet of forty-one pages, plus about twenty pages of Snake Oil Liniment advertisements, is one of the curiosities of cowboy literature. It includes a collection of cowboy songs, the earliest I know of in time of printing, antedating by eleven years Jack Thorp's booklet of cowboy songs printed at Estancia, New Mexico, in 1908. Clark Stanley no doubt used the contents of his pamphlet in medicine show harangues, thus adding to the cowboy myth. As time went on, he added scraps of anecdotes and western history, along with testimonials, to the pamphlet, the latest edition I have seen being about 1906, printed in Worcester, Massachusetts.

STEEDMAN, CHARLES J. *Bucking the Sagebrush,* New York, 1904. OP. Charming; much of nature. Illustrated by Russell.

Charles M. Russell, in *The Virginian* by Owen Wister

STEVENS, MONTAGUE. *Meet Mr. Grizzly*, University of New Mexico Press, Albuquerque, 1943. Stevens, a Cambridge Englishman, ranched, hunted, and made deductions. See characterization under "Bears and Bear Hunters."

STREETER, FLOYD B. *Prairie Trails and Cow Towns*, Boston, 1936. OP. This brings together considerable information on Kansas cow towns. Primary books on the subject, besides those by Stuart Henry, McCoy, Vestal, and Wright herewith listed, are *The Oklahoma Scout*, by Theodore Baughman, Chicago, 1886; *Midnight and Noonday*, by G. D. Freeman, Caldwell, Kansas, 1892; biographies of Wild Bill Hickok, town marshal; Stuart N. Lake's biography of Wyatt Earp, another noted marshal; *Hard Knocks*, by Harry Young, Chicago, 1915, not too prudish to notice dance hall girls but too Victorian to say much. Many Texas trail drivers had trouble as well as fun in the cow towns. *Life and Adventures of Ben Thompson*, by W. M. Walton, 1884, reprinted at Bandera, Texas, 1926, gives samples. Thompson was more gambler than cowboy; various other men who rode from cow camps into town and found themselves in their element were gamblers and gunmen first and cowboys only in passing.

STUART, GRANVILLE. *Forty Years on the Frontier*, two volumes, Cleveland, 1925. Nothing better on the cowboy has ever been written than the chapter entitled "Cattle Business" in Volume II. A prime work throughout. OP.

THORP, JACK (N. Howard) has a secure place in range literature because of his contribution in cowboy songs. (See entry under "Cowboy Songs and Other Ballads.") In 1926 he had printed at Santa Fe a paper-backed book of 123 pages entitled *Tales of the Chuck Wagon,* but "didn't sell more than two or three million copies." Some of the tales are in his posthumously published reminiscences, *Pardner of the Wind* (as told to Neil McCullough Clark, Caxton, Caldwell, Idaho, 1945). This book is richest on range horses, and will be found listed in the section on "Horses."

TOWNE, CHARLES WAYLAND, and WENTWORTH, EDWARD NORRIS. *Shepherd's Empire,* University of Oklahoma Press, Norman, 1945. Not firsthand in the manner of Gilfillan's *Sheep,* nor charming and light in the manner of Kupper's *The Golden Hoof,* but an essayical history, based on research. The deference paid to Mary Austin's *The Flock* marks the author as civilized. Towne wrote the book; Wentworth supplied the information. Wentworth's own book, *America's Sheep Trails,* Iowa State College Press, Ames, 1948, is ponderous, amorphous, and in part, only a eulogistic "mugbook."

TOWNSHEND, R. B. *A Tenderfoot in Colorado,* London, 1923; *The Tenderfoot in New Mexico,* 1924. Delightful as well as faithful. Literature by an Englishman who translated Tacitus under the spires of Oxford after he retired from the range.

TREADWELL, EDWARD F. *The Cattle King,* New York, 1931; reissued by Christopher, Boston. A strong biography of a very strong man—Henry Miller of California.

TRENHOLM, VIRGINIA COLE. *Footprints on the Frontier,* Douglas, Wyoming, 1945. OP. The best range material in this book is a reprint of parts of James C. Shaw's *Pioneering in Texas and Wyoming,* privately printed at Cheyenne in 1931.

TRUETT, VELMA STEVENS. *On the Hoof in Nevada,*

Gehrett-Truett-Hall, Los Angeles, 1950. A 613-page album of cattle brands—priced at $10.00. The introduction is one of the sparse items on Nevada ranching.

TUCKER, PATRICK T. *Riding the High Country*, Caldwell, Idaho, 1933. A brave book with much of Charlie Russell in it. OP.

VESTAL, STANLEY (pen name for Walter S. Campbell). *Queen of Cow Towns, Dodge City*, Harper, New York, 1952. "Bibulous Babylon," "Killing of Dora Hand," and "Marshals for Breakfast" are chapter titles suggesting the tenor of the book.

Vocabulario y Refranero Criollo, text and illustrations by Tito Saudibet, Guillermo Kraft Ltda., Buenos Aires, 1945. North American ranges have called forth nothing to compare with this fully illustrated, thorough, magnificent history-dictionary of the gaucho world. It stands out in contrast to American slapdash, puerile-minded pretenses at dictionary treatises on cowboy life.

"He who knows only the history of his own country does not know it." The cowboy is not a singular type. He was no better rider than the Cossack of Asia. His counterpart in South America, developed also from Spanish cattle, Spanish horses, and Spanish techniques, is the gaucho. Literature on the gaucho is extensive, some of it of a high order. Primary is *Martín Fierro*, the epic by José Hernández (published 1872-79). A translation by Walter Owen was published in the United States in 1936. No combination of knowledge, sympathy, imagination, and craftsmanship has produced stories and sketches about the cowboy equal to those on the gaucho by W. H. Hudson, especially in *Tales of the Pampas* and *Far Away and Long Ago*, and by R. B. Cunninghame Graham, whose writings are dispersed and difficult to come by.

WEBB, WALTER PRESCOTT. *The Great Plains*, Ginn, Boston, 1931. While this landmark in historical interpretation of the West is by no means limited to the subject of grazing, it contains a long and penetrating chapter entitled "The Cattle

Kingdom." The book is an analysis of land, climate, barbed wire, dry farming, wells and windmills, native animal life, etc. No other work on the plains country goes so meatily into causes and effects.

WELLMAN, PAUL I. *The Trampling Herd,* Doubleday, Garden City, N. Y., 1939; reissued, 1951. An attempt to sum up the story of the cattle range in America.

WHITE, STEWART EDWARD. *Arizona Nights,* 1902. "Rawhide," one of the stories in this excellent collection, utilizes folk motifs about rawhide with much skill.

WILLIAMS, J. R. *Cowboys Out Our Way,* with an Introduction by J. Frank Dobie, Scribner's, New York, 1951. An album reproducing about two hundred of the realistic, humorous, and human J. R. Williams syndicated cartoons. This book was preceded by *Out Our Way,* New York, 1943, and includes numerous cartoons therein printed. There was an earlier and less extensive collection. Modest Jim Williams has been progressively dissatisfied with all his cartoon books—and with cartoons not in books. I like them and in my Introduction say why.

WISTER, OWEN. *The Virginian,* 1902. Wister was an outsider looking in. His hero, "The Virginian," is a cowboy without cows—like the cowboys of Eugene Manlove Rhodes; but this hero does not even smell of cows, whereas Rhodes's men do. Nevertheless, the novel authentically realizes the code of the range, and it makes such absorbing reading that in fifty years (1902-52) it sold over 1,600,000 copies, not counting foreign translations and paper reprints.

Wister was an urbane Harvard man, of clubs and travels. In 1952 the University of Wyoming celebrated the fiftieth anniversary of the publication of *The Virginian.* To mark the event, Frances K. W. Stokes wrote *My Father Owen Wister,* a biographical pamphlet including "ten letters written to his mother during his trip to Wyoming in 1885" — a trip that prepared him to write the novel. The pamphlet is published at Laramie, Wyoming, name of publisher not printed on it.

WRIGHT, PETER. *A Three-Foot Stool,* New York and

London, 1909. Like several other Englishmen who went west, Wright had the perspective that enabled him to comprehend some aspects of ranch life more fully than many range men who knew nothing but their own environment and times. He compares the cowboy to the cowherd described by Queen Elizabeth's Spenser. Into exposition of ranching on the Gila, he interweaves talk on Arabian afreets, Stevenson's philosophy of adventure, and German imperialism.

WRIGHT, ROBERT M. *Dodge City, Cowboy Capital,* Wichita, Kansas, 1913; reprinted. Good on the most cowboyish of all the cow towns.

PAMPHLETS

Pamphlets are an important source of knowledge in all fields. No first-class library is without them. Most of them become difficult to obtain, and some bring higher prices than whole sets of books. Of numerous pamphlets pertaining to the range, only a few are listed here. *History of the Chisum War, or Life of Ike Fridge,* by Ike Fridge, Electra, Texas (undated), is as compact as jerked beef and as laconic as conversation in alkali dust. James F. Hinkle, in his *Early Days of a Cowboy on the Pecos,* Roswell, New Mexico, 1937, says: "One noticeable characteristic of the cowpunchers was that they did not talk much." Some people don't have to talk to say plenty. Hinkle was one of them. At a reunion of trail drivers in San Antonio in October, 1928, Fred S. Millard showed me his laboriously written reminiscences. He wanted them printed. I introduced him to J. Marvin Hunter of Bandera, Texas, publisher of *Frontier Times.* I told Hunter not to ruin the English by trying to correct it, as he had processed many of the earth-born reminiscences in *The Trail Drivers of Texas.* He printed Millard's *A Cowpuncher of the Pecos* in pamphlet form shortly thereafter. It begins: "This is a piece I wrote for the Trail Drivers." They would understand some things on which he was not explicit.

About 1940, as he told me, Bob Beverly of Lovington, New Mexico, made a contract with the proprietor of the town's weekly newspaper to print his reminiscences. By the time the contractor had set eighty-seven pages of type he saw that he would lose money if he set any more. He gave Bob Beverly back more manuscript than he had used and stapled a pamphlet entitled *Hobo of the Rangeland*. The philosophy in it is more interesting to me than the incidents. "The cowboy of the old West worked in a land that seemed to be grieving over something—a kind of sadness, loneliness in a deathly quiet. One not acquainted with the plains could not understand what effect it had on the mind. It produced a heartache and a sense of exile."

Crudely printed, but printed as the author talked, is *The End of the Long Horn Trail*, by A. P. (Ott) Black, Selfridge, North Dakota (August, 1939). As I know from a letter from his *compadre*, Black was blind and sixty-nine years old when he dictated his memoirs to a college graduate who had sense enough to retain the flavor. Black's history is badly botched, but reading him is like listening. "It took two coons and an alligator to spend the summer on that cotton plantation. . . . Cowpunchers were superstitious about owls. One who rode into my camp one night had killed a man somewhere and was on the dodge. He was lying down by the side of the campfire when an owl flew over into some hackberry trees close by and started hooting. He got up from there right now, got his horse in, saddled up and rode off into the night."

John Alley is—or was—a teacher. His *Memories of Roundup Days*, University of Oklahoma Press, 1934 (just twenty small pages), is an appraisal of range men, a criticism of life seldom found in old-timers who look back. On the other hand, some pamphlets prized by collectors had as well not have been written. Here is the full title of an example: *An Aged Wanderer, A Life Sketch of J. M. Parker, A Cowboy of the Western Plains in the Early Days.* "Price 40 cents. Headquarters, Elkhorn Wagon Yard, San Angelo, Texas." It was printed about 1923. When Parker wrote it he was senile, and there is no evidence that he was ever possessed of intelligence. The itching to get into print does not guarantee that the itcher has anything worth printing.

Some of the best reminiscences have been pried out of range men. In 1914 the Wyoming Stock Growers Association resolved a Historical Commission into existence. A committee was appointed and, naturally, one man did the work. In 1923 a fifty-five-page pamphlet entitled *Letters from Old Friends and Members of the Wyoming Stock Growers Association* was printed at Cheyenne. It is made up of unusually informing and pungent recollections by intelligent cowmen.

22

Cowboy Songs and Other Ballads

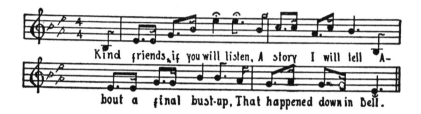

Kind friends, if you will listen, A story I will tell A-bout a final bust-up, That happened down in Dell.

COWBOY SONGS and ballads are generally ranked alongside Negro spirituals as being the most important of America's contributions to folk song. As compared with the old English and Scottish ballads, the cowboy and all other ballads of the American frontiers generally sound cheap and shoddy. Since John A. Lomax brought out his collection in 1910, cowboy songs have found their way into scores of songbooks, have been recorded on hundreds of records, and have been popularized, often—and naturally—without any semblance to cowboy style, by thousands of radio singers. Two general anthologies are recommended especially for the cowboy songs they contain: *American Ballads and Folk Songs,* by John A. and Alan Lomax, Macmillan, New York, 1934; *The American Songbag,* by Carl Sandburg, Harcourt, Brace, New York, 1927.

LARKIN, MARGARET. *Singing Cowboy* (with music), New York, 1931. OP.

LOMAX, JOHN A., and LOMAX, ALAN. *Cowboy Songs and Other Frontier Ballads,* Macmillan, New York, 1938. This is a much added-to and revised form of Lomax's 1910 collection, under the same title. It is the most complete of all anthologies. More than any other man, John A. Lomax is responsible for having made cowboy songs a part of the common heritage of America. His autobiographic *Adventures of a Ballad Hunter* (Macmillan, 1947) is in quality far above the jingles that most cowboy songs are.

Missouri, as no other state, gave to the West and Southwest. Much of Missouri is still more southwestern in character than much of Oklahoma. For a full collection, with full treatment, of the ballads and songs, including bad-man and cowboy songs, sung in the Southwest there is nothing better than *Ozark Folksongs*, collected and edited by Vance Randolph, State Historical Society of Missouri, Columbia, 1946-50. An unsurpassed work in four handsome volumes.

OWENS, WILLIAM A. *Texas Folk Songs*, Southern Methodist University Press, Dallas, 1950. A miscellany of British ballads, American ballads, "songs of doleful love," etc. collected in Texas mostly from country people of Anglo-American stock. Musical scores for all the songs.

The Texas Folklore Society has published many cowboy songs. Its publications *Texas and Southwestern Lore* (1927) and *Follow de Drinkin' Gou'd* (1928) contain scores, with music and anecdotal interpretations. Other volumes contain other kinds of songs, including Mexican.

THORP, JACK (N. Howard). *Songs of the Cowboys*, Boston, 1921. OP. Good, though limited, anthology, without music and with illuminating comments. A pamphlet collection that Thorp privately printed at Estancia, New Mexico, in 1908, was one of the first to be published. Thorp had the perspective of both range and civilization. He was a kind of troubadour himself. The opening chapter, "Banjo in the Cow Camps," of his posthumous reminiscences, *Pardner of the Wind*, is delicious.

23

Horses: Mustangs and Cow Ponies

THE WEST WAS DISCOVERED, battled over, and won by men on horseback. Spanish conquistadores saddled their horses in Vera Cruz and rode until they had mapped the continents from the Horn to Montana and from the Floridas to the harbors of the Californias. The padres with them rode on horseback, too, and made every mission a horse ranch. The national dance of Mexico, the Jarabe, is an interpretation of the clicking of hoofs and the pawing and prancing of spirited horses that the Aztecs noted when the Spaniards came. Likewise, the chief contribution made by white men of America to the folk songs of the world—the cowboy songs—are rhythmed to the walk of horses.

Astride horses introduced by the conquistadores to the Americas, the Plains Indians became almost a separate race from the foot-moving tribes of the East and the stationary Pueblos of the Rockies. The men that later conquered and corralled these wild-riding Plains Indians were plainsmen on horses and cavalrymen. The earliest American explorers and trappers of both Plains and Rocky Mountains went out in the saddle. The first industrial link between the East and the West was a mounted pack train beating out the Santa Fe Trail. On west beyond the end of this trail, in Spanish California, even the drivers of oxen rode horseback. The first transcontinental express was the Pony Express.

Outlaws and bad men were called "long riders." The Texas Ranger who followed them was, according to his own proverb, "no better than his horse." Booted sheriffs from Brownsville on the Rio Grande to the Hole in the Wall in

the Big Horn Mountains lived in the saddle. Climactic of all
the riders rode the cowboy, who lived with horse and herd.

In the Old West the phrase "left afoot" meant nothing
short of being left flat on your back. "A man on foot is no
man at all," the saying went. If an enemy could not take a
man's life, the next best thing was to take his horse. Where
cow thieves went scot free, horse thieves were hanged, and
to say that a man was "as common as a horse thief" was to
express the nadir of commonness. The pillow of the frontiersmen who slept with a six-shooter under it was a saddle,
and hitched to the horn was the loose end of a stake rope.
Just as "Colonel Colt" made all men equal in a fight, the
horse made all men equal in swiftness and mobility.

The proudest names of civilized languages when literally
translated mean "horseman": eques, caballero, chevalier,
cavalier. Until just yesterday the Man on Horseback had
been for centuries the symbol of power and pride. The advent
of the horse, from Spanish sources, so changed the ways and
psychology of the Plains Indians that they entered into what
historians call the Age of Horse Culture. Almost until the
automobile came, the whole West and Southwest were dominated by a Horse Culture.

Material on range horses is scattered through the books
listed under "Range Life," "Stagecoaches, Freighting," "Pony
Express."

No thorough comprehension of the Spanish horse of the
Americas is possible without consideration of this horse's
antecedents, and that involves a good deal of the horse history of the world.

BROWN, WILLIAM ROBINSON. *The Horse of the Desert*
(no publisher or place on title page), 1936; reprinted by
Macmillan, New York. A noble, beautiful, and informing
book.

CABRERA, ANGEL. *Caballos de América*, Buenos Aires,
1945. The authority on Argentine horses.

CARTER, WILLIAM H. *The Horses of the World,* National Geographic Society, Washington, D. C., 1923. A concentrated survey.

Cattleman. Published at Fort Worth, this monthly magazine of the Texas and Southwestern Cattle Raisers Association began in 1939 to issue, for September, a horse number. It has published a vast amount of material both scientific and popular on range horses. Another monthly magazine worth knowing about is the *Western Horseman,* Colorado Springs, Colorado.

DENHARDT, ROBERT MOORMAN. *The Horse of the Americas,* University of Oklahoma Press, Norman, 1947. This historical treatment of the Spanish horse could be better ordered; some sections of the book are little more than miscellanies.

DOBIE, J. FRANK. *The Mustangs,* illustrated by Charles Banks Wilson, Little, Brown, Boston, 1952. Before this handsome book arrives at the wild horses of North America, a third of it has been spent on the Arabian progenitors of the Spanish horse, the acquisition of the Spanish horse by western Indians, and the nature of Indian horses. There are many narratives of mustangs and mustangers and of Spanish-blooded horses under the saddle. The author has tried to compass the natural history of the animal and to blend vividness with learning. The book incorporates his *Tales of the Mustang,* a slight volume published in an edition of only three hundred copies in 1936. It also incorporates a large part of *Mustangs and Cow Horses,* edited by Dobie, Boatright, and Ransom, and issued by the Texas Folklore Society, Austin, 1940 — a volume that went out of print not long after it was published.

DODGE, THEODORE A. *Riders of Many Lands,* New York, 1893. Illustrations by Remington. Wide and informed views.

GRAHAM, R. B. CUNNINGHAME. *The Horses of the Conquest,* London, 1930. Graham was both historian and horseman, as much at home on the pampas as in his ancient Scottish home. This excellent book on the Spanish horses intro-

Charles Banks Wilson, in *The Mustangs*
by J. Frank Dobie (1952)

duced to the Western Hemisphere is in a pasture to itself. Reprinted in 1949 by the University of Oklahoma Press, with introduction and notes by Robert Moorman Denhardt.

GREER, JAMES K. *Bois d'Arc to Barbed Wire*, Dallas, 1936. OP.

HASTINGS, FRANK. *A Ranchman's Recollections*, Chicago, 1921. "Old Gran'pa" is close to the best American horse story I have ever read. OP.

HAYES, M. HORACE. *Points of the Horse*, London, 1904. This and subsequent editions are superior in treatment and illustrations to earlier editions. Hayes was a far traveler and scholar as well as horseman. One of the less than a dozen best books on the horse.

JAMES, WILL. *Smoky*, Scribner's, New York, 1930. Perhaps the best of several books that Will James — always with illustrations — has woven around horse heroes.

LEIGH, WILLIAM R. *The Western Pony*, New York, 1933. One of the most beautifully printed books on the West; beautiful illustrations; illuminating text. OP.

MULLER, DAN. *Horses*, Reilly and Lee, Chicago, 1936. Interesting illustrations.

PATTULLO, GEORGE. *The Untamed*, New York, 1911. A collection of short stories, among which "Corazon" and "Neutria" are excellent on horses. OP.

PERKINS, CHARLES ELLIOTT. *The Pinto Horse*, Santa Barbara, California, 1927. A fine narrative, illustrated by Edward Borein. OP.

RIDGEWAY, W. *The Origin and Influence of the Thoroughbred Horse*, Cambridge, England, 1905. A standard work, though many of its conclusions are disputed, especially by Lady Wentworth in her *Thoroughbred Racing Stock and Its Ancestors*, London, 1938.

SANTEE, ROSS. *Men and Horses*, New York, 1926. Three chapters of this book, "A Fool About a Horse," "The Horse Wrangler," and "The Rough String," are especially recommended. *Cowboy*, New York, 1928, reveals in a fine way the rapport between the cowboy and his horse. *Sleepy Black*,

New York, 1933, is a story of a horse designed for younger readers; being good on the subject, it is good for any reader. All OP.

SIMPSON, GEORGE GAYLOR. *Horses: The Story of the Horse Family in the Modern World and through Sixty Million Years of History,* Oxford University Press, New York, 1951. In the realm of paleontology this work supplants all predecessors. Bibliography.

STEELE, RUFUS. *Mustangs of the Mesas,* Hollywood, California, 1941. OP. Modern mustanging in Nevada; excellently written narratives of outstanding mustangs.

STONG, PHIL. *Horses and Americans,* New York, 1939. A survey and a miscellany combined. OP.

Charles M. Russell, in *The Untamed*
by George Pattullo (1911)

THORP, JACK (N. Howard) as told to Neil McCullough Clark. *Pardner of the Wind,* Caxton, Caldwell, Idaho, 1945. Two chapters in this book make the "Spanish thunderbolts," as Jack Thorp called the mustangs and Spanish cow horses, graze, run, pitch, and go gentle ways as free as the wind. "Five Hundred Mile Horse Race" is a great story. No other range man excepting Ross Santee has put down so much everyday horse lore in such a fresh way.

TWEEDIE, MAJOR GENERAL W. *The Arabian Horse: His Country and People,* Edinburgh and London, 1894. One of the few horse books to be classified as literature. Wise in the blend of horse, land, and people.

WENTWORTH, LADY. *The Authentic Arabian Horse and His Descendants,* London, 1945. Rich in knowledge and both magnificent and munificent in illustrations. Almost immediately after publication, this noble volume entered the rare book class.

WYMAN, WALKER D. *The Wild Horse of the West,* Caxton, Caldwell, Idaho, 1945. A scholarly sifting of virtually all available material on mustangs. Readable. Only thorough bibliography on subject so far published.

24

The Bad Man Tradition

PLENTY of six-shooter play is to be found in most of the books about old-time cowboys; yet hardly one of the professional bad men was a representative cowboy. Bad men of the West and cowboys alike wore six-shooters and spurs; they drank each other's coffee; they had a fanatical passion for liberty — for themselves. But the representative cowboy was a reliable hand, hanging through drought, blizzard, and high water to his herd, whereas the bona fide bad man lived on the dodge. Between the killer and the cowboy standing up for his rights or merely shooting out the lights for fun, there was as much difference as between Adolf Hitler and Winston Churchill. Of course, the elements were mixed in the worst of the bad men, as they are in the best of all good men. No matter what deductions analysis may lead to, the fact remains that the western bad men of open range days have become a part of the American tradition. They represent six-shooter culture at its zenith — the wild and woolly side of the West — a stage between receding bowie knife individualism of the backwoods and blackguard, machine-gun gangsterism of the city.

The songs about Sam Bass, Jesse James, and Billy the Kid reflect popular attitude toward the hard-riding outlaws. Sam Bass, Jesse James, Billy the Kid, the Daltons, Cole Younger, Joaquin Murrieta, John Wesley Hardin, Al Jennings, Belle Starr, and other "long riders" with their guns in their hands have had their biographies written over and over. They were not nearly as immoral as certain newspaper columnists lying under the cloak of piety. As time goes on, they, like antique

Tom Lea: Pancho Villa, in *Southwest Review* (1951)

Robin Hood and the late Pancho Villa, recede from all realistic judgment. If the picture show finds in them models for generosity, gallantry, and fidelity to a code of liberty, and if the public finds them picturesque, then philosophers may well be thankful that they lived, rode, and shot.

"The long-tailed heroes of the revolver," to pick a phrase from Mark Twain's unreverential treatment of them in *Roughing It,* often did society a service in shooting each other — aside from providing entertainment to future generations. As "The Old Cattleman" of Alfred Henry Lewis' *Wolfville* stories says, "A heap of people need a heap of killing." Nor can the bad men be logically segregated from the long-haired killers on the side of the law like Wild Bill Hickok and Wyatt Earp. W. H. Hudson once advanced the theory that bloodshed and morality go together. If American civilization proceeds, the rage for collecting books on bad men will probably subside until a copy of Miguel Antonio Otero's *The Real Billy the Kid* will bring no higher price than a first edition of A. Edward Newton's *The Amenities of Book-Collecting.*

See "Fighting Texians," "Texas Rangers," "Range Life," "Cowboy Songs and Other Ballads."

AIKMAN, DUNCAN. *Calamity Jane and the Lady Wildcats,* 1927. OP. Patronizing in the H. L. Mencken style.

BILLY THE KID. We've got to take him seriously, not so much for what he was —

> There are twenty-one men I have put bullets through,
> And Sheriff Pat Garrett must make twenty-two —

as for his provocations. Popular imagination, represented by writers of all degrees, goes on playing on him with cumulative effect. As a figure in literature the Kid has come to lead the whole field of western bad men. The *Saturday Review,* for October 11, 1952, features a philosophical essay entitled "Billy the Kid: Faust in America—The Making of a Legend." The growth of this legend is minutely traced through a period of seventy-one years (1881-1952) by J. C. Dykes in *Billy the Kid: The Bibliography of a Legend,* University of New Mexico Press, Albuquerque, 1952 (186 pages). It lists 437 titles, including magazine pieces, mimeographed plays, motion pictures, verses, pamphlets, fiction. In a blend of casualness and scholarship, it gives the substance and character of each item. Indeed, this bibliography reads like a continued story, with constant references to both antecedent and subsequent action. Pat Garrett, John Chisum, and other related characters weave all through it. A first-class bibliography that is also readable is almost a new genre.

Pat F. Garrett, sheriff of Lincoln County, New Mexico, killed the Kid about midnight, July 14, 1881. The next spring his *Authentic Life of Billy the Kid* was published at Santa Fe, at least partly written, according to good evidence, by a newspaperman named Ash Upton. This biography is one of the rarities in Western Americana. In 1927 it was republished by Macmillan, New York, under title of *Pat F. Garrett's Authentic Life of Billy the Kid,* edited by Maurice G. Fulton. This is now OP but remains basic. The most widely circulated biography has been *The Saga of Billy the Kid* by Walter Noble Burns, New York, 1926. It contains a deal of fictional conversation and it has no doubt contributed to the Robin-Hoodizing of the lethal character baptized as William H. Bonney, who was born in New York in 1859 and now lives with undiminished vigor as Billy the Kid. Walter Noble Burns was not so successful with *The Robin Hood of El Dorado: The Saga of Joaquin Murrieta* (1932), or, despite its hogsheads of blood, with *Tombstone* (1927).

CANTON, FRANK M. *Frontier Trails,* Boston, 1930.

COE, GEORGE W. *Frontier Fighter,* Boston, 1934; reprinted by University of New Mexico Press, Albuquerque. The autobiography of one of Billy the Kid's men as recorded by Nan Hillary Harrison.

COOLIDGE, DANE. *Fighting Men of the West,* New York, 1932. Biographical sketches. OP.

CUNNINGHAM, EUGENE. *Triggernometry*, 1934; reprinted by Caxton, Caldwell, Idaho. Excellent survey of codes and characters. Written by a man of intelligence and knowledge. Bibliography.

FORREST, E. R. *Arizona's Dark and Bloody Ground*, Caxton, Caldwell, Idaho, 1936.

GARD, WAYNE. *Sam Bass*, Boston, 1936. Most of the whole truth. OP.

HALEY, J. EVETTS. *Jeff Milton — A Good Man with a Gun*, University of Oklahoma Press, Norman, 1949. Jeff Milton the whole man as well as the queller of bad men.

HENDRICKS, GEORGE. *The Bad Man of the West*, Naylor, San Antonio, 1941. Analyses and classifications go far toward making this treatment of old subjects original. Excellent bibliographical guide.

HOUGH, EMERSON. *The Story of the Outlaw*, 1907. OP. An omnibus carelessly put together with many holes in it.

LAKE, STUART. *Wyatt Earp*, Boston, 1931. Best written of all gunmen biographies. Earp happened to be on the side of the law.

LANKFORD, N. P. *Vigilante Days and Ways*, 1890, 1912. OP. Full treatment of lawlessness in the Northwest.

LOVE, ROBERTUS. *The Rise and Fall of Jesse James*, New York, 1926. Excellently written. OP.

RAINE, WILLIAM McLEOD. *Famous Sheriffs and Western Outlaws*, Doubleday, Garden City, N. Y., 1929. A rogues' gallery. *Guns of the Frontier*, Boston, 1940. Another miscellany. OP.

RASCOE, BURTON. *Belle Starr*, New York, 1941. OP.

RIPLEY, THOMAS. *They Died with Their Boots On*, 1935. Mostly about John Wesley Hardin. OP.

SABIN, EDWIN L. *Wild Men of the Wild West*, New York, 1929. Biographic survey of killers from the Mississippi to the Pacific. OP.

WILD BILL HICKOK. The subject of various biographies, among them those by Frank J. Wilstach (1926) and William

E. Connelley (1933). The *Nebraska History Magazine* (Volume X) for April-June 1927 is devoted to Wild Bill and contains a "descriptive bibliography" on him by Addison E. Sheldon.

WOODHULL, FROST. "Folk-Lore Shooting," in *Southwestern Lore*, Publication IX of the Texas Folklore Society, 1931. Rich. Humor.

25

Mining and Oil

DURING the twentieth century oil has brought so much money to the Southwest that the proceeds from cattle have come to look like tips. This statement is not based on statistics, though statistics no doubt exist — even on the cost of catching sun perch. Geological, legal, and economic writings on oil are mountainous in quantity, but the human drama of oil yet remains, for the most part, to be written. It is odd to find such a modern book as Erna Fergusson's *Our Southwest* not mentioning oil. It is odd that no book of national reputation comes off the presses about any aspect of oil. The nearest to national notice on oil is the daily report of transactions on the New York Stock Exchange. Oil companies subsidize histories of themselves, endow universities with money to train technicians they want, control state legislatures and senates, and dictate to Congress what they want for themselves in income tax laws; but so far they have not been able to hire anybody to write a book about oil that anybody but the hirers themselves wants to read. Probably they don't read them. The first thing an oilman does after amassing a few millions is buy a ranch on which he can get away from oil — and on which he can spend some of his oil money.

People live a good deal by tradition and fight a good deal by tradition also, voting more by prejudice. When one considers the stream of cow country books and the romance of mining living on in legends of lost mines and, then, the desert of oil books, one realizes that it takes something more than money to make the mare of romance run. Geology and economics are beyond the aim of this *Guide,* but if oil money keeps on buying up ranch land, the history of modern ranching will be resolved into the biographies of a comparatively few oilmen.

BOATRIGHT, MODY C. *Gib Morgan: Minstrel of the Oil Fields.* Texas Folklore Society, Austin, 1945. Folk tales about Gib rather than minstrelsy. OP.

BOONE, LALIA PHIPPS. *The Petroleum Dictionary,* University of Oklahoma Press, Norman, 1952. "More than 6,000 entries: definitions of technical terms and everyday expressions, a comprehensive guide to the language of the oil industry."

CAUGHEY, JOHN WALTON. *Gold Is the Cornerstone* (1948). Adequate treatment of the discovery of California gold and of the miners. *Rushing for Gold* (1949). Twelve essays by twelve writers, with emphasis on travel to California. Both books published by University of California Press, Berkeley and Los Angeles.

CENDRARS, BLAISE. *Sutter's Gold,* London, 1926. OP.

CLARK, JAMES A., and HALBOUTY, MICHEL T. *Spindletop,* Random House, New York, 1952. On January 10, 1901, the Spindletop gusher, near Beaumont, Texas, roared in the oil age. This book, while it presumes to record what Pat Higgins was thinking as he sat in front of a country store, seems to be "the true story." The bare facts in it make drama.

DE QUILLE, DAN (pseudonym for William Wright). *The Big Bonanza,* Hartford, 1876. Reprinted, 1947. OP.

DOBIE, J. FRANK. *Coronado's Children,* Dallas, 1930; reprinted by Grosset and Dunlap, New York. Legendary tales of lost mines and buried treasures of the Southwest. *Apache Gold and Yaqui Silver,* Little, Brown, Boston, 1939. More of the same thing.

EMRICH, DUNCAN, editor. *Comstock Bonanza,* Vanguard, New York, 1950. A collection of writings, garnered mostly from West Coast magazines and newspapers, bearing on mining in Nevada during the boom days of Mark Twain's

Tom Lea, in *Santa Rita* by Martin W. Schwettmann
(1943)

Roughing It. James G. Gally's writing is a major discovery in a minor field.

FORBES, GERALD. *Flush Production: The Epic of Oil in the Gulf-Southwest,* University of Oklahoma Press, Norman, 1942.

GILLIS, WILLIAM R. *Goldrush Days with Mark Twain,* New York, 1930. OP.

GLASSCOCK, LUCILLE. *A Texas Wildcatter,* Naylor, San

Antonio, 1952. The wildcatter is Mrs. Glasscock's husband. She chronicles this player's main moves in the game and gives an insight into his energy-driven ambition.

HOUSE, BOYCE. *Oil Boom,* Caxton, Caldwell, Idaho, 1941. With Boyce House's earlier *Were You in Ranger?,* this book gives a contemporary picture of the gushing days of oil, money, and humanity.

LYMAN, GEORGE T. *The Saga of the Comstock Lode,* 1934, and *Ralston's Ring,* 1937. Both published by Scribner's, New York.

McKENNA, JAMES A. *Black Range Tales,* New York, 1936. Reminiscences of prospecting life. OP.

MATHEWS, JOHN JOSEPH. *Life and Death of an Oilman: The Career of E. W. Marland,* University of Oklahoma Press, Norman, 1951. Mature in style and in interpretative power, John Joseph Mathews goes into the very life of an oilman who was something else.

RISTER, C. C. *Oil! Titan of the Southwest,* University of Oklahoma Press, Norman, 1949. Facts in factual form. Plenty of oil wealth and taxes; nothing on oil government.

SHINN, CHARLES H. *Mining Camps,* 1885, reprinted by Knopf, New York, 1948. Perhaps the most competent analysis extant on the behavior of the gold hunters, with emphasis on their self-government. *The Story of the Mine as Illustrated by the Great Comstock Lode of Nevada,* New York, 1896. OP. Shinn knew and he knew also how to combine into form.

STUART, GRANVILLE. *Forty Years on the Frontier,* Cleveland, 1925. Superb on California and Montana hunger for precious metals. OP.

TAIT, SAMUEL W. *Wildcatters: An Informal History of Oil-Hunting in America,* Princeton University Press, 1946. OP.

TWAIN, MARK. *Roughing It.* The mining boom itself.

26

Nature; Wild Life; Naturalists

"NO MAN," says Mary Austin, "has ever really entered into the heart of any country until he has adopted or made up myths about its familiar objects." A man might reject the myths but he would have to know many facts about its natural life and have imagination as well as knowledge before entering into a country's heart. The history of any land begins with nature, and all histories must end with nature.

"The character of a country is the destiny of its people," wrote Harvey Fergusson in *Rio Grande*. Ross Calvin, also of New Mexico, had the same idea in mind when he entitled his book *Sky Determines*. "Culture mocks at the boundaries set up by politics," Clark Wissler said. "It approaches geographical boundaries with its hat in its hand." The engineering of water across mountains, electric translation of sounds, refrigeration of air and foods, and other technical developments carry human beings a certain distance across some of nature's boundaries, but no cleverness of science can escape nature. The inhabitants of Yuma, Arizona, are destined forever to face a desert devoid of graciousness. Technology does not create matter; it merely uses matter in a skilful way—uses it up.

Man advances by learning the secrets of nature and taking advantage of his knowledge. He is deeply happy only when in harmony with his work and environments. The backwoodsman, early settler, pioneer plainsman, mountain man were all like some infuriated beast of Promethean capabilities tearing at its own vitals. Driven by an irrational energy, they seemed intent on destroying not only the growth of the soil but the power of the soil to reproduce. Davy Crockett, the great bear killer, was "wrathy to kill a bear," and as respects bears and other wild life, one may search the chronicles of his kind in vain for anything beyond the incidents of chase and slaughter. To quote T. B. Thorpe's blusterous bear hunter, the whole matter may be summed up in one sentence: "A bear is started and he is killed." For the average American of the soil, whether wearing out a farm, shotgunning with a headlight the last doe of a woodland, shooting the last buffalo on the range, trapping the last howling lobo, winging the last prairie chicken, running down in an automobile the last antelope, making a killer's target of any hooting owl or flying heron that comes within range, poisoning the last eagle to fly over a sheep pasture—for him the circumstances of the killing have expressed his chief intellectual interest in nature.

A sure sign of advancing civilization has been the rapidly changing popular attitude toward nature during recent years. People are becoming increasingly interested not merely in conserving game for sportsmen to shoot, but in preserving all wild life, in observing animals, in cultivating native flora, in building houses that harmonize with climate and land-scape. Roger Tory Peterson's *Field Guide to the Birds* has become one of the popular standard works of America.

The story of the American Indian is—despite taboos and squalor—a story of harmonizations with nature. "Wolf Brother," in *Long Lance*, by Chief Buffalo Child Long Lance, is a poetic concretion of this harmony. As much at ease with the wilderness as any Blackfoot Indian was George Frederick Ruxton, educated English officer and gentleman, who rode horseback from Vera Cruz to the Missouri River and wrote *Adventures in Mexico and the Rocky Mountains*. In this book he tells how a lobo followed him for days from camp to camp, waiting each evening for his share of fresh meat and some-times coming close to the fire at night. Any orthodox American would have shot the lobo at first appearance. Ruxton had the civilized perspective on nature represented by Thoreau and Saint Francis of Assisi. Primitive harmony was run over by frontier wrath to kill, a wrath no less barbaric than primitive superstitions.

But the coyote's howl is more tonic than all theories about nature; the buck's whistle more invigorating; the bull's bellow in the canyon more musical; the call of the bobwhite more serene; the rattling of the rattlesnake more logical; the scream of the panther more arousing to the imagination; the odor from the skunk more lingering; the sweep of the buzzard in the air more majestical; the wariness of the wild turkey brighter; the bark of the prairie dog lighter; the guesses of the armadillo more comical; the upward dartings and dippings of the scissortail more lovely; the flight of the sandhill cranes more fraught with mystery.

There is an abundance of printed information on the animal life of America, to the west as well as to the east. Much of it cannot be segregated; the earthworm, on which Darwin wrote a book, knows nothing of regionalism. The best books on nature come from and lead to the Grasshopper's Library, which is free to all consultants. I advise the consultant to listen to the owl's hoot for wisdom, plant nine bean rows for peace, and, with Wordsworth, sit on an old gray stone listening for "authentic tidings of invisible things." Studies are only to "perfect nature." In the words of Mary Austin, "They that make the sun noise shall not fail of the sun's full recompense."

Like knowledge in any other department of life, that on nature never comes to a stand so long as it has vitality. A continuing interest in natural history is nurtured by *Natural History*, published by the American Museum of Natural History, New York; *Nature*, published in Washington, D. C.; *The Living Wilderness*, also from Washington; *Journal of Mammalogy*, a quarterly, Baltimore, Maryland; *Audubon Magazine* (formerly *Bird Lore*), published by the National Audubon Society, New York; *American Forests*, Washington, D. C., and various other publications.

In addition to books of natural history interest listed below, others are listed under "Buffaloes and Buffalo Hunters," "Bears and Bear Hunters," "Coyotes, Lobos, and Panthers," "Birds and Wild Flowers," and "Interpreters." Perhaps a majority of worthy books pertaining to the western half of America look on the outdoors.

ADAMS, W. H. DAVENPORT (from the French of Benedict Revoil). *The Hunter and the Trapper of North America,* London, 1875. A strange book.

ARNOLD, OREN. *Wild Life in the Southwest,* Dallas, 1936. Helpful chapters on various characteristic animals and plants. OP.

BAILEY, VERNON. *Mammals of New Mexico,* United States Department of Agriculture, Bureau of Biological Survey, Washington, D. C., 1931. *Biological Survey of Texas,* 1905. OP. The "North American Fauna Series," to which these two books belong, contains or points to the basic facts covering most of the mammals of the Southwest.

BAILLIE-GROHMAN, WILLIAM A. *Camps in the Rockies,* 1882. A true sportsman, Baillie-Grohman was more interested in living animals than in just killing. OP.

BEDICHEK, ROY. *Adventures with a Texas Naturalist,* Doubleday, Garden City, N. Y., 1947. To be personal, Roy Bedichek has the most richly stored mind I have ever met; it is as active as it is full. Liberal in the true sense of the word, it frees other minds. Here, using facts as a means, it gives meanings to the hackberry tree, limestone, mockingbird, Inca dove, Mexican primrose, golden eagle, the Davis Mountains, cedar cutters, and many another natural phenomenon. *Adventures with a Texas Naturalist* is regarded by some good judges as the wisest book in the realm of natural history produced in America since Thoreau wrote.

The title of Bedichek's second book, *Karánkaway Country* (Garden City, 1950), is misleading. The Karankawa Indians start it off, but it goes to coon inquisitiveness, prairie chicken dances, the extinction of species to which the whooping crane is approaching, browsing goats, dignified skunks, swifts in love flight, a camp in the brush, dust, erosion, silt— always with thinking added to seeing. The foremost naturalist of the Southwest, Bedichek constantly relates nature to civilization and human values.

BROWNING, MESHACH. *Forty-Four Years of the Life of a Hunter*, 1859; reprinted, Philadelphia, 1928. Prodigal on bear and deer.

CAHALANE, VICTOR H. *Mammals of North America*, Macmillan, New York, 1947. The author is a scientist with an open mind on the relationships between predators and game animals. His thick, delightfully illustrated book is the best dragnet on American mammals extant. It contains excellent lists of references.

CATON, JUDGE JOHN DEAN. *Antelope and Deer of America*, 1877. Standard work. OP.

DOBIE, J. FRANK. *The Longhorns* (1941) and *The Mustangs* (1952), while hardly to be catalogued as natural history books, go farther into natural history than most books on cattle and horses go. *On the Open Range* (1931; reprinted by Banks Upshaw, Dallas) contains a number of animal stories more or less true. Ben Lilly of *The Ben Lilly Legend* (Boston, 1950) thought that God had called him to hunt. He spent his life, therefore, in hunting. He saw some things in nature beyond targets.

DODGE, RICHARD I. *The Hunting Grounds of the Great West*, London, 1877. Published in New York the same year under title of *The Plains of the Great West and Their Inhabitants*. Outstanding survey of outstanding wild creatures.

DUNRAVEN, EARL OF. *The Great Divide*, London, 1876; reprinted under title of *Hunting in the Yellowstone*, 1925. OP.

ELLIOTT, CHARLES (editor). *Fading Trails*, New York, 1942. Humanistic review of characteristic American wild life. OP.

FLACK, CAPTAIN. *The Texas Ranger, or Real Life in the Backwoods,* 1866; another form of *A Hunter's Experience in the Southern States of America,* by Captain Flack, "The Ranger," London, 1866.

GANSON, EVE. *Desert Mavericks,* Santa Barbara, California, 1928. Illustrated; delightful. OP.

GEISER, SAMUEL WOOD. *Naturalists of the Frontier,* Southern Methodist University Press, Dallas, 1937; revised and enlarged edition, 1948. Biographies of men who were characters as well as scientists, generally in environments alien to their interests.

GERSTAECKER, FREDERICK. *Wild Sports in the Far West,* 1854. A translation from the German. Delightful reading and revealing picture of how backwoodsmen of the Mississippi Valley "lived off the country."

GRAHAM, GID. *Animal Outlaws,* Collinsville, Oklahoma, 1938. OP. A remarkable collection of animal stories. Privately printed.

GRINNELL, GEORGE BIRD. Between 1893 and 1913, Grinnell, partly in collaboration with Theodore Roosevelt, edited five volumes for The Boone and Crockett Club that contain an extraordinary amount of information, written mostly by men of civilized perspective, on bears, deer, mountain sheep, buffaloes, cougars, elk, wolves, moose, mountains, and forests. The series, long out of print, is a storehouse of knowledge not to be overlooked by any student of wild life in the West. The titles are: *American Big-Game Hunting,* 1893; *Hunting in Many Lands,* 1895; *Trail and Camp-Fire,* 1897; *American Big Game in Its Haunts,* 1904; *Hunting at High Altitudes,* 1913.

GRINNELL, JOSEPH; DIXON, JOSEPH S.; and LINSDALE, JEAN M. *Fur-Bearing Mammals of California: Their Natural History, Systematic Status, and Relation to Man,* two volumes, University of California Press, Berkeley, 1937. The king, so far, of all state natural histories.

HALL, E. RAYMOND. *Mammals of Nevada,* University of California Press, Berkeley and Los Angeles, 1946. So far as my knowledge goes, this is the only respect-worthy book extant pertaining to the state whose economy is based on fees from divorces and gambling and whose best-known citizen is Senator Pat McCarran.

HARTMAN, CARL G. *Possum,* University of Texas Press, Austin, 1952. This richly illustrated book comprehends

Charles M. Russell, in *The Blazed Trail of the Old Frontier* by Agnes C. Laut (1926)

everything pertaining to the subject from prehistoric marsupium to baking with sweet potatoes in a Negro cabin. It is the outcome of a lifetime's scientific investigation not only of possums but of libraries and popular talk. Thus, in addition to its biographical and natural history aspects, it is a study in the evolution of man's knowledge about one of the world's folkiest creatures.

HORNADAY, WILLIAM T. *Camp Fires on Desert and Lava,* London, n.d. OP. Dr. Hornaday, who died in 1937, was the first director of the New York Zoological Park. He was a great conservationist and an authority on the wild life of America.

HUDSON, W. H. *The Naturalist in La Plata,* New York, 1892. Not about the Southwest or even North America, but

Hudson's chapters on "The Puma," "Some Curious Animal Weapons," "The Mephitic Skunk," "Humming Birds," "The Strange Instincts of Cattle," "Horse and Man," etc. come home to the Southwest. Few writers tend to make readers so aware; no other has written so delightfully of the lands of grass.

INGERSOLL, ERNEST. *Wild Neighbors,* New York, 1897. OP. A superior work. Chapter II, "The Father of Game," is on the cougar; Chapter IV, "The Hound of the Plains," is on the coyote; there is an excellent essay on the badger. Each chapter is provided with a list of books affording more extended treatment of the subject.

JAEGER, EDMUND C. *Denizens of the Desert,* Boston, 1922. OP. "Don Coyote," the roadrunner, and other characteristic animals. *Our Desert Neighbors,* Stanford University Press, California, 1950.

LOCKE, LUCIE H. *Naturally Yours, Texas,* Naylor, San Antonio, 1949. Charm must never be discounted; it is far rarer than facts, and often does more to lead to truth. This slight book is in verse and drawings, type integrated with delectable black-and-white representations of the prairie dog, armadillo, sanderling, mesquite, whirlwind, sand dune, mirage, and dozens of other natural phenomena. The only other book in this list to which it is akin is Eve Ganson's *Desert Mavericks.*

LUMHOLTZ, CARL. *Unknown Mexico,* New York, 1902. Nearly anything about animals as well as about Indians and mountains of Mexico may be found in this extraordinary two-volume work. OP.

MCILHENNY, EDWARD A. *The Alligator's Life History,* Boston, 1935. OP. The alligator got farther west than is generally known—at least within reach of Laredo and Eagle Pass on the Rio Grande. McIlhenny's book treats—engagingly, intimately, and with precision—of the animal in Louisiana. Hungerers for anatomical biology are referred to *The Alligator and Its Allies* by A. M. Reese, New York, 1915. I have more to say about McIlhenny in Chapter 30.

MARCY, COLONEL R. B. *Thirty Years of Army Life on the Border,* New York, 1866. Marcy had a scientific mind and a high sense of values. He knew how to write and what he wrote remains informing and pleasant.

MARTIN, HORACE T. *Castorologia, or The History and Traditions of the Canadian Beaver,* London, 1892. OP. The beaver is a beaver, whether on Hudson's Bay or the Mexican side of the Rio Grande. Much has been written on this animal, the propeller of the trappers of the West, but this famous book remains the most comprehensive on facts and the amplest in conception. The author was humorist as well as scientist.

MENGER, RUDOLPH. *Texas Nature Observations and Reminiscences,* San Antonio, 1913. OP. Being of an educated German family, Dr. Menger found many things in nature more interesting than two-headed calves.

MILLS, ENOS. *The Rocky Mountain Wonderland, Wild Life on the Rockies, Waiting in the Wilderness,* and other books. Some naturalists have taken exception to some observations recorded by Mills; nevertheless, he enlarges and freshens mountain life.

MUIR, JOHN. *The Mountains of California, Our National Parks,* and other books. Muir, a great naturalist, had the power to convey his wise sympathies and brooded-over knowledge.

MURPHY, JOHN MORTIMER. *Sporting Adventures in the Far West,* London, 1879. One of the earliest roundups of game animals of the West.

NEWSOME, WILLIAM M. *The Whitetailed Deer,* New York, 1926. OP. Standard work.

PALLISER, JOHN. *The Solitary Hunter; or Sporting Adventures in the Prairies,* London, 1857.

ROOSEVELT, THEODORE. *Outdoor Pastimes of an American Hunter,* with a chapter entitled "Books on Big Game"; *Hunting Adventures in the West; The Wilderness Hunter; Ranch Life and the Hunting Trail; A Book Lover's Holiday in the Open; The Deer Family* (in collaboration).

SEARS, PAUL B. *Deserts on the March,* University of Oklahoma Press, Norman, 1935. Dramatic picturization of the forces of nature operating in what droughts of the 1930's caused to be called "the Dust Bowl." "Drought and Wind and Man" might be another title.

SETON, ERNEST THOMPSON. *Wild Animals I Have Known; Lives of the Hunted.* Probably no other writer of America has aroused so many people, young people especially, to an interest in our wild animals. Natural history encyclopedias he has authored are *Life Histories of Northern Animals,* New York, 1920, and *Lives of Game Animals,* New York, 1929. Seton's final testament, *Trail of an Artist Naturalist* (Scribner's, New York, 1941), has a deal on wild life of the Southwest.

THORPE, T. B. *The Hive of the Bee-Hunter,* New York, 1854. OP. Juicy.

WARREN, EDWARD ROYAL. *The Mammals of Colorado,* University of Oklahoma Press, Norman, 1942. OP.

27

Buffaloes and Buffalo Hunters

THE LITERATURE on the American bison, more popularly called buffalo, is enormous. Nearly everything of consequence pertaining to the Plains Indians touches the animal. The relationship of the Indian to the buffalo has nowhere been better stated than in Note 49 to the Benavides *Memorial,* edited by Hodge and Lummis. "The Great Buffalo Hunt at Standing Rock," a chapter in *My Friend the Indian* by James McLaughlin, sums up the hunting procedure; other outstanding treatments of the buffalo in Indian books are to be found in *Long Lance* by Chief Buffalo Child Long Lance; *Letters and Notes on . . . the North American Indians* by George Catlin; *Forty Years a Fur Trader* by Charles Larpenteur. Floyd B. Streeter's chapter on "The Buffalo Range" in *Prairie Trails and Cow Towns* lists twenty-five sources of information.

The bibliography that supersedes all other bibliographies is in the book that supersedes all other books on the subject — Frank Gilbert Roe's *The North American Buffalo.* More about it in the list that follows.

Nearly all men who got out on the plains were "wrathy to kill" buffaloes above all else. The Indians killed in great numbers but seldom wastefully. The Spaniards were restrained by Indian hostility. Mountain men, emigrants crossing the plains, Santa Fe traders, railroad builders, Indian fighters, settlers on the edge of the plains, European sportsmen, all slaughtered and slew. Some observed, but the average American hunter's observations on game animals are about as illuminating as the trophy-stuffed den of a rich oilman or the

Harold D. Bugbee: Buffaloes

lockers of a packing house. Lawrence of Arabia won his name through knowledge and understanding of Arabian life and through power to lead and to write. Buffalo Bill won his name through power to exterminate buffaloes. He was a buffalo man in the way that Hitler was a Polish Jew man.

It is a pleasure to note the writings of sportsmen with inquiring minds and of scientists and artists who hunted. Three examples are: *The English Sportsman in the Western Prairies*, by the Hon. Grantley F. Berkeley, London, 1861; *Travels in the Interior of North America, 1833-1834*, by

Maximilian, Prince of Wied (original edition, 1843), included in that "incomparable storehouse of buffalo lore from early eye-witnesses," *Early Western Travels*, edited by Reuben Gold Thwaites; George Catlin's *Letters and Notes on the Manners, Customs and Conditions of the North American Indians*, London, 1841.

Three aspects of the buffalo stand out: the natural history of the great American animal; the interrelationship between Indian and buffalo; the white hunter—and exterminator.

ALLEN, J. A. *The American Bison, Living and Extinct*, Cambridge, Mass., 1876. Reprinted in 9th Annual Report of the United States Geological and Geographical Survey, Washington, 1877. Basic and rich work, much of it appropriated by Hornaday.

BRANCH, E. DOUGLAS. *The Hunting of the Buffalo*, New York, 1925. Interpretative as well as factual. OP.

COOK, JOHN R. *The Border and the Buffalo*, Topeka, Kansas, 1907. Personal narrative.

DIXON, OLIVE. *Billy Dixon*, Guthrie, Oklahoma, 1914; reprinted, Dallas, 1927. Bully autobiography; excellent on the buffalo hunter as a type. OP.

DODGE, R. I. *The Plains of the Great West and Their Inhabitants*, New York, 1877. One of the best chapters of this source book is on the buffalo.

GARRETSON, MARTIN S. *The American Bison*, New York Zoological Society, New York, 1938. Not thorough, but informing. Limited bibliography. OP.

GRINNELL, GEORGE BIRD (1849-1938) may be classed next to J. A. Allen and W. T. Hornaday as historian of the buffalo. His primary sources were the buffaloed plains and the Plains Indians, whom he knew intimately. "In Buffalo Days" is a long and excellent essay by him in *American Big-Game Hunting*, edited by Theodore Roosevelt and George Bird Grinnell, New York, 1893. He has another long essay, "The Bison," in *Musk-Ox, Bison, Sheep and Goat* by Caspar

Whitney, George Bird Grinnell, and Owen Wister, New York, 1904. His noble and beautifully simple *When Buffalo Ran,* New Haven, 1920, is specific on work from a buffalo horse. Again in his noble two-volume work on *The Cheyenne Indians* (1923) Grinnell is rich not only on the animal but on the Plains Indian relationship to it. All OP.

HALEY, J. EVETTS. *Charles Goodnight, Cowman and Plainsman,* 1936. Goodnight killed and also helped save the buffalo. Haley has preserved his observations.

HORNADAY, W. T. *Extermination of the American Bison* (Smithsonian Reports for 1887, published in 1889, Part II). Hornaday was a good zoölogist but inferior in research.

INMAN, HENRY. *Buffalo Jones' Forty Years of Adventure,* Topeka, Kansas, 1899. A book rich in observations as well as experience, though Jones was a poser. OP.

LAKE, STUART N. *Wyatt Earp,* Boston, 1931. Early chapters excellent on buffalo hunting.

McCREIGHT, M. I. *Buffalo Bone Days,* Sykesville, Pa., 1939. OP. A pamphlet strong on buffalo bones, for fertilizer.

PALLISER, JOHN (and others). *Journals, Detailed Reports, and Observations, relative to Palliser's Exploration of British North America, 1857-1860,* London, 1863. According to Frank Gilbert Roe, "a mine of inestimable information" on the buffalo.

Panhandle-Plains Historical Review, Canyon, Texas. Articles and reminiscences, *passim.*

PARKMAN, FRANCIS. *The Oregon Trail,* 1847. Available in various editions, this book contains superb descriptions of buffaloes and prairies.

POE, SOPHIE A. *Buckboard Days* (edited by Eugene Cunningham), Caldwell, Idaho, 1936. Early chapters. OP.

ROE, FRANK GILBERT. *The North American Buffalo,* University of Toronto Press, 1951. A monumental work comprising and critically reviewing virtually all that has been written on the subject and supplanting much of it. No other scholar dealing with the buffalo has gone so fully into the subject or viewed it from so many angles, brought out so many aspects of natural history and human history. In a field where ignorance has often prevailed, Roe has to be iconoclastic in order to be constructive. If his words are sometimes sharp, his mind is sharper. The one indispensable book on the subject.

RYE, EDGAR. *The Quirt and the Spur*, Chicago, 1909. Rye was in the Fort Griffin, Texas, country when buffalo hunters dominated it. OP.

SCHULTZ, JAMES WILLARD. *Apauk, Caller of Buffalo*, New York, 1916. OP. Whether fiction or nonfiction, as claimed by the author, this book realizes the relationships between Plains Indian and buffalo.

WEEKES, MARY. *The Last Buffalo Hunter* (as told by Norbert Welsh), New York, 1939. OP. The old days recalled with upspringing sympathy. Canada—but buffaloes and buffalo hunters were pretty much the same everywhere.

West Texas Historical Association (Abilene, Texas) *Year Books*. Reminiscences and articles, *passim*.

WILLIAMS, O. W. A privately printed letter of eight unnumbered pages, dated from Fort Stockton, Texas, June 30, 1930, containing the best description of a buffalo stampede that I have encountered. It is reproduced in Dobie's *On the Open Range*.

28

Bears and Bear Hunters

THE BEAR, whether black or grizzly, is a great American citizen. Think of how many children have been put to sleep with bear stories! Facts about the animal are fascinating; the effect he has had on the minds of human beings associated with him transcends naturalistic facts. The tree on which Daniel Boone carved the naked fact that here he "Killed A. Bar In the YEAR 1760" will never die. Davy Crockett killed 105 bars in one season, and his reputation as a bar hunter, plus ability to tell about his exploits, sent him to Congress. He had no other reason for going. The grizzly was the hero of western tribes of Indians from Alaska on down into the Sierra Madre. Among western white men who met him, occasionally in death, the grizzly inspired a mighty saga, the cantos of which lie dispersed in homely chronicles and unrecorded memories as well as in certain vivid narratives by Ernest Thompson Seton, Hittell's John Capen Adams, John G. Neihardt, and others.

For all that, neither the black bear nor the grizzly has been amply conceived of as an American character. The conception must include a vast amount of folklore. In a chapter on "Bars and Bar Hunters" in *On the Open Range* and in "Juan Oso" and "Under the Sign of Ursa Major," chapters of *Tongues of the Monte*, I have indicated the nature of this dispersed epic in folk tales.

In many of the books listed under "Nature; Wild Life; Naturalists" and "Mountain Men" the bear "walks like a man."

ALTER, J. CECIL. *James Bridger*, Salt Lake City, 1925; reprinted by Long's College Book Co., Columbus, Ohio. Contains several versions of the famous Hugh Glass bear story.

HITTELL, THEODORE H. *The Adventures of John Capen Adams*, 1860; reprinted 1911, New York. OP. Perhaps no man has lived who knew grizzlies better than Adams. A rare personal narrative.

MILLER, JOAQUIN. *True Bear Stories*, Chicago, 1900. OP. Truth questionable in places; interest guaranteed.

MILLER, LEWIS B. *Saddles and Lariats*, Boston, 1909. OP. The chapter "In a Grizzly's Jaws" is a wonderful bear story.

MILLS, ENOS A. *The Grizzly, Our Greatest Wild Animal*, Houghton Mifflin, Boston, 1919. Some naturalists have accused Mills of having too much imagination. He saw much and wrote vividly.

NEIHARDT, JOHN G. *The Song of Hugh Glass*, New York, 1915. An epic in vigorous verse of the West's most famous man-and-bear story. This imagination-rousing story has been told over and over, by J. Cecil Alter in *James Bridger*, by Stanley Vestal in *Mountain Men*, and by other writers.

ROOSEVELT, THEODORE. *Hunting Adventures in the*

Charles M. Russell, in *Fifteen Thousand Miles by Stage*
by Carrie Adell Strahorn (1915)

West (1885) and *The Wilderness Hunter* (1893)—books reprinted in parts or wholly under varying titles. Several narratives of hunts intermixed with baldfaced facts.

SETON, ERNEST THOMPSON. *The Biography of a Grizzly,* 1900; now published by Appleton-Century-Crofts, New York. *Monarch, the Big Bear of Tallac,* 1904. Graphic narratives.

SKINNER, M. P. *Bears in the Yellowstone,* Chicago, 1925. OP. A naturalist's rounded knowledge, pleasantly told.

STEVENS, MONTAGUE. *Meet Mr. Grizzly,* University of New Mexico Press, Albuquerque, 1943. Montague Stevens graduated from Trinity College, Cambridge, in 1881 and came to New Mexico to ranch. As respects deductions on observed data, his book is about the most mature yet published by a ranchman. Goodnight experienced more, had a more ample nature, but he lacked the perspective, the mental training, to know what to make of his observations. Another English rancher, R. B. Townshend, had perspective and charm but was not a scientific observer. So far as sense of smell goes, *Meet Mr. Grizzly* is as good as W. H. Hudson's *A Hind in Richmond Park.* On the nature and habits of grizzly bears, it is better than *The Grizzly* by Enos Mills.

WRIGHT, WILLIAM H. *The Grizzly Bear: The Narrative of a Hunter-Naturalist, Historical, Scientific and Adventurous,* New York, 1928. OP. This is not only the richest and justest book published on the grizzly; it is among the best books of the language on specific mammals. Wright had a passion for bears, for their preservation, and for arousing informed sympathy in other people. Yet he did not descend to propaganda. His *The Black Bear,* London, n.d., is good but no peer to his work on the grizzly. Also OP.

29

Coyotes, Lobos, and Panthers

I SEPARATE COYOTES, lobos, and panthers from the mass of animals because they, along with bears, have made such an imprint on human imagination. White-tailed deer are far more common and more widely dispersed. Men, women also, by the tens of thousands go out with rifles every fall in efforts to get near them; but the night-piercing howl and the cunning ways of the coyote, the panther's track and the rumor of his scream have inspired more folk tales than all the deer.

Lore and facts about these animals are dispersed in many books not classifiable under natural history. Lewis and Clark and nearly all the other chroniclers of Trans-Mississippi America set down much on wild life. James Pike's *Scout and Ranger* details the manner in which, he says, a panther covered him up alive, duplicating a fanciful and delightful tale in Gerstaecker's *Wild Sports in the Far West*. James B. O'Neil concludes *They Die but Once* with some "Bedtime Stories" that—almost necessarily—bring in a man-hungry panther.

COYOTES AND LOBOS

The two full-length books on Brother Coyote listed below specify most of the printed literature on the animal. (He is "Brother" in Mexican tales and I feel much more brotherly toward him than I feel toward character assassins in political power.) It would require another book to catalogue in detail all the writings that include folk tales about Don Coyote. Ethnologists and scientific folklorists recognize what they call "the Coyote Circle" in the folklore of many tribes of Indians.

Morris Edward Opler in *Myths and Legends of the Lipan Apache Indians,* 1940, and in *Myths and Tales of the Chiricahua Apache Indians,* 1942 (both issued by the American Folklore Society, New York) treats fully of this cycle. Numerous tales that belong to the cycle are included by J. Gilbert McAllister, an anthropologist who writes as a humanist, in his extended collection, "Kiowa-Apache Tales," in *The Sky Is My Tipi,* edited by Mody C. Boatright for the Texas Folklore Society (Publication XXII), Southern Methodist University Press, Dallas, 1949.

Literary retellers of Indian coyote folk tales have been many. The majority of retellers from western Indians include Coyote. One of the very best is Frank B. Linderman, in *Indian Why Stories* and *Indian Old-Man Stories.* These titles are substantive: *Old Man Coyote* by Clara Kern Bayliss (New York, 1908, OP), *Coyote Stories* by Mourning Dove (Caldwell, Idaho, 1934, OP); *Don Coyote* by Leigh Peck (Boston, 1941) gets farther away from the Indian, is more juvenile. The *Journal of American Folklore* and numerous Mexican books have published hundreds of coyote folk tales from Mexico. Among the most pleasingly told are *Picture Tales from Mexico* by Dan Storm, 1941 (Lippincott, Philadelphia). The first two writers listed below bring in folklore.

CUSHING, FRANK HAMILTON. *Zuñi Breadstuff,* Museum of the American Indian, Heye Foundation, New York, 1920. This extraordinary book, one of the most extraordinary ever written on a particular people, is not made up of coyote lore alone. In it the coyote becomes a character of dignity and destiny, and the telling is epic in dignity as well as in prolongation. Frank Hamilton Cushing was a genius; his sympathy, insight, knowledge, and mastery of the art of writing enabled him to reveal the spirit of the Zuñi Indians as almost no other writer has revealed the spirit of any other tribe. Their attitude toward Coyote is beautifully developed. Cushing's *Zuñi Folk Tales* (Knopf, New York, 1901, 1931) is climactic on "tellings" about Coyote.

DOBIE, J. FRANK. *The Voice of the Coyote*, Little, Brown, Boston, 1949. Not only the coyote but his effect on human imagination and ecological relationships. Natural history and folklore; many tales from factual trappers as well as from Mexican and Indian folk. This is a strange book in some ways. If the author had quit at the end of the first chapter, which is on coyote voicings and their meaning to varied listeners, he would still have said something. The book includes some, but by no means all, of the material on the subject in *Coyote Wisdom* (Publication XIV of the Texas Folklore Society, 1938) edited by J. Frank Dobie and now distributed by Southern Methodist University Press, Dallas.

GRINNELL, GEORGE BIRD. "Wolves and Wolf Nature," in *Trail and Camp-Fire*, New York, 1897. This long chapter is richer in facts about the coyote than anything published prior to *The Voice of the Coyote*, which borrows from it extensively.

LOFBERG, LILA, and MALCOLMSON, DAVID. *Sierra Outpost*, Duell, Sloan and Pearce, New York, 1941. An extraordinary detailment of the friendship between two people, isolated by snow high in the California Sierras, and three coyotes. Written with fine sympathy, minute in observations.

MATHEWS, JOHN JOSEPH. *Talking to the Moon*, University of Chicago Press, 1945. A wise and spiritual interpretation of the black-jack country of eastern Oklahoma, close to the Osages, in which John Joseph Mathews lives. Not primarily about coyotes, the book illuminates them more than numerous books on particular animals illuminate their subjects.

MURIE, ADOLPH. *Ecology of the Coyote in the Yellowstone*, United States Government Printing Office, Washington, D. C., 1940. An example of strict science informed by civilized humanity. *The Wolves of Mount McKinley*, United States Government Printing Office, Washington, D. C., 1944. Murie's combination of prolonged patience, science, and sympathy behind the observations has never been common. His ecological point of view is steady. Highly interesting reading.

YOUNG, STANLEY PAUL (with Edward A. Goldman). *The Wolves of North America,* American Wildlife Institute, Washington, D. C., 1944. Full information, full bibliography, without narrative power. *Sketches of American Wildlife,* Monumental Press, Baltimore, 1946. This slight book contains pleasant chapters on the Puma, Wolf, Coyote, Antelope and other animals characteristic of the West. (With Hartley H. T. Jackson) *The Clever Coyote,* Stackpole, Harrisburg, Pa., and Wildlife Management Institute, Washington, D. C., 1951. Emphasis upon the economic status and control of the species, an extended classification of subspecies, and a full bibliography make this book and Dobie's *The Voice of the Coyote* complemental to each other rather than duplicative.

PANTHERS

Anybody who so wishes may call them mountain lions. Where there were Negro mammies, white children were likely to be haunted in the night by fear of ghosts. Otherwise, for some children of the South and West, no imagined terror of the night equaled the panther's scream. The Anglo-American lore pertaining to the panther is replete with stories of attacks on human beings. Indian and Spanish lore, clear down to where W. H. Hudson of the pampas heard it, views the animal as *un amigo de los cristianos*—a friend of man. The panther is another animal as interesting for what people associated with him have taken to be facts as for the facts themselves.

BARKER, ELLIOTT S. *When the Dogs Barked 'Treed',* University of New Mexico Press, Albuquerque, 1946. Mainly on mountain lions, but firsthand observations on other predatory animals also. Before he became state game warden, the author was for years with the United States Forest Service.

HIBBEN, FRANK C. *Hunting American Lions,* New York, 1948; reprinted by University of New Mexico Press, Albuquerque. Mr. Hibben considers hunting panthers and bears a terribly dangerous business that only intrepid heroes like himself would undertake. Sometimes in this book, but more awesomely in *Hunting American Bears,* he manages to out-zane Zane Grey, who had to warn his boy scout readers and puerile-minded readers of added years that *Roping Lions in the Grand Canyon* is true in contrast to the fictional *Young Lion Hunter,* which uses some of the same material.

HUDSON, W. H. *The Naturalist in La Plata,* New York, 1892. A chapter in this book entitled "The Puma, or Lion of America" provoked an attack from Theodore Roosevelt (in *Outdoor Pastimes of an American Hunter*); but it remains the most delightful narrative-essay yet written on the subject.

YOUNG, STANLEY PAUL, and GOLDMAN, EDWARD A. *The Puma, Mysterious American Cat,* American Wildlife Institute, Washington, D. C., 1946. Scientific, liberal with information of human interest, bibliography. We get an analysis of the panther's scream but it does not curdle the blood.

30

Birds and Wild Flowers

NEARLY EVERYBODY ENJOYS to an extent the singing of birds and the colors of flowers; to the majority, however, the enjoyment is casual, generalized, vague, in the same category as that derived from a short spell of prattling by a healthy baby. Individuals who study birds and native flora experience an almost daily refreshment of the spirit and growth of the intellect. For them the world is an unending Garden of Delight and a hundred-yard walk down a creek that runs through town or pasture is an exploration. Hardly anything beyond good books, good pictures and music, and good talk is so contributory to the enrichment of life as a sympathetic knowledge of the birds, wild flowers, and other native fauna and flora around us.

The books listed are dominantly scientific. Some include keys to identification. Once a person has learned to use the key for identifying botanical or ornithological species, he can spend the remainder of his life adding to his stature.

BIRDS

BAILEY, FLORENCE MERRIAM. *Birds of New Mexico*, 1928. OP. Said by those who know to be at the top of all state bird books. Much on habits.

BEDICHEK, ROY. *Adventures with a Texas Naturalist* (1947) and *Karánkaway Country* (1950), Doubleday, Garden City, N. Y. These are books of essays on various aspects of nature, but nowhere else can one find an equal amount of penetrating observation on chimney swifts, Inca doves, swallows, golden eagles, mockingbirds, herons, prairie chickens, whooping cranes, swifts, scissortails, and some other birds. As Bedichek writes of them they become integrated with all life.

BRANDT, HERBERT. *Arizona and Its Bird Life,* Bird Research Foundation, Cleveland, 1951. This beautiful, richly illustrated volume of 525 pages lives up to its title; the birds belong to the Arizona country, and with them we get pines, mesquites, cottonwoods, John Slaughter's ranch, the north-ward-flowing San Pedro, and many other features of the land. Herbert Brandt's *Texas Bird Adventures,* illustrated by George Miksch Sutton (Cleveland, 1940), is more on the Big Bend country and ranch country to the north than on birds, though birds are here.

DAWSON, WILLIAM LEON. *The Birds of California,* San Diego, etc., California, 1923. OP. Four magnificent volumes, full in illustrations, special observations on birds, and scientific data.

DOBIE, J. FRANK, who is no more of an ornithologist than he is a geologist, specialized on an especially characteristic bird of the Southwest and gathered its history, habits, and folklore into a long article: "The Roadrunner in Fact and Folklore," in *In the Shadow of History,* Publication XV of the Texas Folklore Society, Austin, 1939. OP. "Bob More: Man and Bird Man," *Southwest Review,* Dallas, Vol. XXVII, No. 1 (Autumn, 1941).

NICE, MARGARET MORSE. *The Birds of Oklahoma,* Norman, 1931. OP. United States Biological Survey publication.

OBERHOLSER, HARRY CHURCH. "The Birds of Texas" in manuscript form. "A stupendous work, the greatest of its genre, by the nation's outstanding ornithologist, who has been fifty years making it." The quotation is condensed from an essay by Roy Bedichek in the *Southwest Review,* Dallas, Vol. XXXVIII, No. 1 (Winter, 1953). Maybe some day some man or woman with means will see the light of civilized patriotism and underwrite the publication of these great volumes. Patriotism that does not act to promote the beautiful, the true, and the good had better pipe down.

PETERSON, ROGER TORY. *A Field Guide to Western Birds* (1941) and *A Field Guide to the Birds* (birds of the eastern United States, revised 1947), Houghton Mifflin, Boston. These are standard guides for identification. The range, habits, and characteristics of each bird are summarized.

SIMMONS, GEORGE FINLEY. *Birds of the Austin Region*, University of Texas Press, Austin, 1925. A very thorough work, including migratory as well as nesting species.

SUTTON, GEORGE MIKSCH. *Mexican Birds*, illustrated with water-color and pen-and-ink drawings by the author, University of Oklahoma Press, Norman, 1951. The main part of this handsome book is a personal narrative—pleasant to read even by one who is not a bird man—of discovery in Mexico. To it is appended a résumé of Mexican bird life for the use of other seekers. Sutton's *Birds in the Wilderness: Adventures of an Ornithologist* (Macmillan, New York, 1936) contains essays on pet roadrunners, screech owls, and other congenial folk of the Big Bend of Texas. *The Birds of Brewster County, Texas,* in collaboration with Josselyn Van Tyne, is a publication of the Museum of Zoology, University of Michigan, University of Michigan Press, Ann Arbor, 1937.

Wild Turkey. Literature on this national bird is enormous. Among books I name first *The Wild Turkey and Its Hunting*, by Edward A. McIlhenny, New York, 1914. OP. McIlhenny was a singular man. His family settled on Avery Island, Louisiana, in 1832; he made it into a famous refuge for wild fowls. The memories of individuals of a family long established on a country estate go back several lifetimes. In two books of Negro folklore and in *The Alligator's Life History*, McIlhenny wrote as an inheritor. Initially, he was a hunter-naturalist, but scientific enough to publish in the *Auk* and the *Journal of Heredity*. Age, desire for knowledge, and practice in the art of living dimmed his lust for hunting and sharpened his interest in natural history. His book on the wild turkey, an extension into publishable form of a manuscript from a civilized Alabama hunter, is delightful and illuminative reading.

The Wild Turkey of Virginia, by Henry S. Mosby and Charles O. Handley, published by the Commission of Game and Inland Fisheries of Virginia, Richmond, 1943, is written from the point of view of wild life management. It contains an extensive bibliography. Less technical is *The American Wild Turkey,* by Henry E. Davis, Small Arms Technical Company, Georgetown, South Carolina, 1949. No strain, or subspecies, of the wild turkey is foreign to any other, but human blends in J. Stokley Ligon, naturalist, are unique. The title of his much-in-little book is *History and Management of Merriam's Wild Turkey,* New Mexico Game and Fish Commission, through the University of New Mexico Press, Albuquerque, 1946.

WILD FLOWERS AND GRASSES

The scientific literature on botany of western America is extensive. The list that follows is for laymen as much as for botanists.

BENSON, LYMAN, and DARROW, ROBERT A. *A Manual of Southwestern Desert Trees and Shrubs,* Biological Science Bulletin No. 6, University of Arizona, Tucson, 1944. A thorough work of 411 pages, richly illustrated, with general information added to scientific description.

CARR, WILLIAM HENRY. *Desert Parade: A Guide to Southwestern Desert Plants and Wildlife,* Viking, New York, 1947.

CLEMENTS, FREDERIC E. and EDITH S. *Rocky Mountain Flowers,* H. W. Wilson, New York, 1928. Scientific description, with glossary of terms and key for identification.

COULTER, JOHN M. *Botany of Western Texas,* United States Department of Agriculture, Washington, 1891-94. OP. Nothing has appeared during the past sixty years to take the place of this master opus.

GEISER, SAMUEL WOOD. *Horticulture and Horticultur-*

ists in Early Texas, Southern Methodist University Press, Dallas, 1945. Historical-scientific, more technical than the author's *Naturalists of the Frontier.*

JAEGER, EDMUND C. *Desert Wild Flowers,* Stanford University Press, California, 1940, revised 1947. Scientific but designed for use by any intelligent inquirer.

LUNDELL, CYRUS L., and collaborators. *Flora of Texas,* Southern Methodist University Press, Dallas, 1942- . A "monumental" work, highly technical, being published part by part.

MCKELVEY, SUSAN DELANO. *Yuccas of the Southwestern United States,* Harvard University Press, Cambridge, 1938. Definitive work in two volumes.

Range Plant Handbook, prepared by the Forest Service of the United States Department of Agriculture. United States Government Printing Office, Washington, 1937. A veritable encyclopedia, illustrated.

SCHULZ, ELLEN D. *Texas Wild Flowers,* Chicago, 1928. Good as a botanical guide and also for human uses; includes lore on many plants. OP. *Cactus Culture,* Orange Judd, New York, 1932. Now in revised edition.

SILVIUS, W. A. *Texas Grasses,* published by the author, San Antonio, 1933. A monument, of 782 illustrated pages, to a lifetime's disinterested following of knowledge "like a star."

STEVENS, WILLIAM CHASE. *Kansas Wild Flowers,* University of Kansas Press, Lawrence, 1948. This is more than a state book, and the integration of knowledge, wisdom, and appreciation of flower life with botanical science makes it appeal to layman as well as to botanist. 463 pages, 774 illustrations. Applicable to the whole plains area.

STOCKWELL, WILLIAM PALMER, and BREAZEALE, LUCRETIA. *Arizona Cacti,* Biological Science Bulletin No. 1, University of Arizona, Tucson, 1933. Beautifully illustrated.

THORNBER, JOHN JAMES, and BONKER, FRANCES. *The Fantastic Clan: The Cactus Family,* New York, 1932. OP.

THORP, BENJAMIN CARROLL. *Texas Range Grasses,* Uni-

versity of Texas Press, Austin, 1952. A survey of 168 species
of grasses, their adaptability to soils and regions, and their
values for grazing. Beautifully illustrated and printed, but no
index.

WHITEHOUSE, EULA. *Texas Wild Flowers in Natural
Colors*, 1936; republished 1948 in Dallas. OP. Toward 200
flowers are pictured in colors, each in conjunction with descriptive material. The finding lists are designed to enable
novices to identify flowers. A charming book.

Paisano (roadrunner) means
fellow-countryman

31

Negro Folk Songs and Tales

WEST OF A WAVERING line along the western edge of the central parts of Texas and Oklahoma the Negro is not an important social or cultural element of the Southwest, just as the modern Indian hardly enters into Texas life at all and the Mexican recedes to the east. Negro folk songs and tales of the Southwest have in treatment been blended with those of the South. Dorothy Scarborough's *On the Trail of Negro Folk-Songs* (1925, OP) derives mainly from Texas, but in making up the body of a Negro song, Miss Scarborough says, "You may find one bone in Texas, one in Virginia and one in Mississippi." Leadbelly, a guitar player equally at home in the penitentiaries of Texas and Louisiana, furnished John A. and Alan Lomax with *Negro Folk Songs as Sung by Leadbelly,* New York, 1936 (OP). The Lomax anthologies, *American Ballads and Folk Songs,* 1934, and *Our Singing Country,* 1941 (Macmillan, New York) and Carl Sandburg's *American Songbag* (Harcourt, Brace, New York, 1927) all give the Negro of the Southwest full representation.

Three books of loveliness by R. Emmett Kennedy, *Black Cameos* (1924), *Mellows* (1925), and *More Mellows* (1931) represent Louisiana Negroes. All are OP. An excellent all-American collection is James Weldon Johnson's *Book of American Negro Spirituals,* Viking, New York, 1940. Bibliographies and lists of other books will be found in *The Negro and His Songs* (1925, OP) and *Negro Workaday Songs,* by Howard W. Odum and Guy B. Johnson, University of North Carolina Press, Chapel Hill, 1926, and in *American Negro Folk-Songs,* by Newman I. White, Cambridge, 1928.

A succinct guide to Negro lore is *American Folk Song and Folk Lore: A Regional Bibliography*, by Alan Lomax and Sidney R. Crowell, New York, 1942. OP.

Narrowing the field down to Texas, J. Mason Brewer's "Juneteenth," in *Tone the Bell Easy*, Publication X of the Texas Folklore Society, Austin, 1932, is outstanding as a collection of tales. In volume after volume the Texas Folklore Society has published collections of Negro songs and tales, A. W. Eddins, Martha Emmons, Gates Thomas, and H. B. Parks being principal contributors.

32

Fiction – Including Folk Tales

FROM THE DAYS of the first innocent sensations in Beadle's Dime Novel series, on through Zane Grey's mass production and up to any present-day newsstand's crowded shelf of *Ace High* and *Flaming Guns* magazines, the Southwest, along with all the rest of the West, has been represented in a fictional output quantitatively stupendous. Most of it has betrayed rather than revealed life, though not with the contemptible contempt for both audience and subject that characterizes most of Hollywood's pictures on the same times, people, and places. Certain historical aspects of the fictional betrayal of the West may be found in E. Douglas Branch's *The Cowboy and His Interpreters*, in *The House of Beadle and Adams and Its Dime and Nickel Novels*, by Albert Johannsen in two magnificent volumes, and in Jay Monaghan's *The Great Rascal: The Life and Adventures of Ned Buntline*, Buntline having been perhaps the most prolific of all Wild West fictionists.

Some "Westerns" have a kind of validity. If a serious reader went through the hundreds of titles produced by William McLeod Raine, Dane Coolidge, Eugene Cunningham, B. M. Bower, the late Ernest Haycox, and other manufacturers of range novels who have known their West at firsthand, he would find, spottedly, a surprising amount of truth about land and men, a fluency in genuine cowboy lingo, and a respect for the code of conduct. Yet even these novels have added to the difficulty that serious writing in the Western field has in getting a hearing on literary, rather than merely Western, grounds. Any writer of Westerns must, like all

178

other creators, be judged on his own intellectual development. "The Western and Ernest Haycox," by James Fargo,
in *Prairie Schooner*, XXVI (Summer, 1952) has something
on this subject.

Actualities in the Southwest seem to have stifled fictional
creation. No historical novel dealing with Texas history has
achieved the drama of the fall of the Alamo or the drawing of
the black beans, has presented a character with half the reality of Sam Houston, Jim Bowie, or Sallie Skull, or has cap-
tured the flavor inherent in the talk on many a ranch gallery.

Historical fiction dealing with early day Texas is, however, distinctly maturing. As a dramatization of Jim Bowie
and the bowie knife, *The Iron Mistress*, by Paul Wellman
(Doubleday, Garden City, New York, 1951), is the best
novel published so far dealing with a figure of the Texas
revolution. In *Divine Average* (Little, Brown, Boston, 1952),
Elithe Hamilton Kirkland weaves from her seasoned knowledge of life and from "realities of those violent years in Texas
history between 1838 and 1858" a story of human destiny.
She reveals the essential nature of Range Templeton more
distinctly, more mordantly, than history has revealed the
essential nature of Sam Houston or any of his contempo-
raries. The wife and daughter of Range Templeton are the
most plausible women in any historical novel of Texas that
I have read. The created world here is more real than
the actual.

Among the early tale-tellers of the Southwest are Jere-
miah Clemens, who wrote *Mustang Gray*, Mollie E. Moore
Davis, of plantation tradition, Mayne Reid, who dared convey real information in his romances, Charles W. Webber, a
naturalist, and T. B. Thorpe, creator of "The Big Bear of
Arkansas."

Fiction that appeared before World War I can hardly be
called modern. No fiction is likely to appear, however, that
will do better by certain types of western character and
certain stages of development in western society than that

produced by Bret Harte, with his gamblers, stage drivers, and mining camps; O. Henry with his "Heart of the West" types; Alfred Henry Lewis with his "Wolfville" anecdotes and characters; Owen Wister, whose *Virginian* remains the classic of cowboy novels without cows; and Andy Adams, whose *Log of a Cowboy* will be read as long as people want a narrative of cowboys sweating with herds.

The authors listed below are in alphabetical order. Those who seem to me to have a chance to survive are not exactly in that order.

FRANK APPLEGATE (died 1932) wrote only two books, *Native Tales of New Mexico* and *Indian Stories from the Pueblos*, but as a delighted and delightful teller of folk tales his place is secure.

MARY AUSTIN seems to be settling down as primarily an expositor. Her novels are no longer read, but the simple tales in *One-Smoke Stories* (her last book, 1934) and in some nonfiction collections, notably *Lost Borders* and *The Flock*, do not recede with time.

While the Southwest can hardly claim Willa Cather, of Nebraska, her *Death Comes for the Archbishop* (1927), which is made out of New Mexican life, is not only the best-known novel concerned with the Southwest but one of the finest of America.

Despite the fact that it is not on the literary map, Will Levington Comfort's *Apache* (1931) remains for me the most moving and incisive piece of writing on Indians of the Southwest that I have found.

If a teller of folk tales and plotless narratives belongs in this chapter, then J. Frank Dobie should be mentioned for the folk tales in *Coronado's Children, Apache Gold and Yaqui Silver,* and *Tongues of the Monte,* also for some of his animal tales in *The Voice of the Coyote,* outlaw and maverick narratives in *The Longhorns,* and "The Pacing White Steed of the Prairies" and other horse stories in *The Mustangs.*

The characters in Harvey Fergusson's *Wolf Song* (1927) are the Mountain Men of Kit Carson's time, and the city of their soul is rollicky Taos. It is a lusty, swift song of the pristine earth. Fergusson's *The Blood of the Conquerors* (1921) tackles the juxtaposition of Spanish-Mexican and Anglo-American elements in New Mexico, of which state he is a native. *Grant of Kingdom* (1950) is strong in wisdom about life, vitality of character, and historical values.

FRED GIPSON's *Hound-Dog Man* and *The Home Place* lack the critical attitude toward life present in great fiction but they are as honest and tonic as creek bottom soil and the people in them are genuine.

FRANK GOODWYN's *The Magic of Limping John* (New York, 1944, OP) is a coherence of Mexican characters, folk tales, beliefs, and ways in the ranch country of South Texas. There is something of magic in the telling, but Frank Goodwyn has not achieved objective control over imagination or sufficiently stressed the art of writing.

PAUL HORGAN of New Mexico has in *The Return of the Weed* (short stories), *Far from Cibola,* and other fiction coped with modern life in the past-haunted New Mexico.

OLIVER LaFARGE's *Laughing Boy* (1929) grew out of the author's ethnological knowledge of the Navajo Indians. He achieves character.

TOM LEA's *The Brave Bulls* (1949) has, although it is a sublimation of the Mexican bullfighting world, Death and Fear of Death for its dominant theme. It may be compared in theme with Stephen Crane's *The Red Badge of Courage.* It is written with the utmost of economy, and is beautiful in its power. *The Wonderful Country* (1952), a historical novel of the frontier, but emphatically not a "Western," recognizes more complexities of society. Its economy and directness parallel the style of Tom Lea's drawings and paintings, with which both books are illustrated.

Sundown, by John Joseph Mathews (1934), goes more profoundly than *Laughing Boy* into the soul of a young Indian (an Osage) and his people. Its translation of the "long,

long thoughts" of the boy and then of "shades of the prison house" closing down upon him is superb writing. The "shades of the prison house" come from oil, with all of the world's coarse thumbs that go with oil.

GEORGE SESSIONS PERRY's *Hold Autumn in Your Hand* (1941) incarnates a Texas farm hand too poor "to flag a gut-wagon," but with the good nature, dignity, and independence of the earth itself. *Walls Rise Up* (1939) is a kind of *Crock of Gold*, both whimsical and earthy, laid on the Brazos River.

KATHERINE ANNE PORTER is as dedicated to artistic perfection as was A. E. Housman. Her output has, therefore, been limited: *Flowering Judas* (1930, enlarged 1935); *Pale Horse, Pale Rider* (1939), *The Leaning Tower* (1944). Her stories penetrate psychology, especially the psychology of a Mexican hacienda, with rare finesse. Her small canvases sublimate the inner realities of men and women. She appeals only to cultivated taste, and to some tastes no other fiction writer in America today is her peer in subtlety.

EUGENE MANLOVE RHODES died in 1934. Most of his novels—distinguished by intricate plots and bright dialogue—had appeared in the *Saturday Evening Post*. His finest story is "Pasó Por Aquí," published in the volume entitled *Once in the Saddle* (1927). Gene Rhodes, who has a canyon—on which he ranched—named for him in New Mexico, was an artist; at the same time, he was a man akin to his land and its men. He is the only writer of the range country who has been accorded a biography—*The Hired Man on Horseback*, by May D. Rhodes, his wife. See under "Range Life."

CONRAD RICHTER's *The Sea of Grass* (1937) is a kind of prose poem, beautiful and tragic. Lutie, wife of the owner of the grass, is perhaps the most successful creation of a ranch woman that fiction has so far achieved.

DOROTHY SCARBOROUGH's *The Wind* (1925) excited the wrath of chambers of commerce and other boosters in West Texas—a tribute to its realism.

The Grapes of Wrath, by John Steinbeck (1939), made Okies a word in the American language. Although dated by the Great Depression, its humanity and realism are beyond date. It is among the few good novels produced by America in the first half of the twentieth century.

JOHN W. THOMASON, after fighting as a marine in World War I, wrote *Fix Bayonets* (1926), followed by *Jeb Stuart* (1930). A native Texan, he followed the southern tradition rather than the western. *Lone Star Preacher* (1941) is a strong and sympathetic characterization of Confederate fighting men woven into fictional form.

In *High John the Conqueror* (Macmillan, 1948) John W. Wilson conveys real feeling for the tragic life of Negro sharecroppers in the Brazos bottoms. He represents the critical awareness of life that has come to modern fiction of the Southwest, in contrast to the sterile action, without creation of character, in most older fiction of the region.

33

Poetry and Drama

"KNOWLEDGE itself is power," Sir Francis Bacon wrote in classical Latin, and in abbreviated form the proverb became a familiar in households and universities alike. But knowledge of what? There is no power in knowledge of mediocre verse.

> I had rather flunk my Wasserman test
> Than read a poem by Edgar A. Guest.

The power of great poetry lies not in knowledge of it but in assimilation of it. Most talk about poetry is vacuous. Poetry can pass no power into any human being unless it itself has power—power of beauty, truth, wit, humor, pathos, satire, worship, and other attributes, always through form. No poor poetry is worth reading. Taste for the best makes the other kind insipid.

Compared with America's best poetry, most poetry of the Southwest is as mediocre as American poetry in the mass is as compared with the great body of English poetry between Chaucer and Masefield. Yet mediocre poetry is not so bad as mediocre sculpture. The mediocre in poetry is merely fatuous; in sculpture, it is ugly. Generations to come will have to look at Coppini's monstrosity in front of the Alamo; it can't rot down or burn up. Volumes of worthless verse, most of it printed at the expense of the versifiers, hardly come to sight, and before long they disappear from existence except for copies religiously preserved in public libraries.

Weak fiction goes the same way. But a good deal of very bad prose in the nonfiction field has some value. In an otherwise dull book there may be a solitary anecdote, an isolated observation on a skunk, a single gesture of some human being otherwise highly unimportant, one salty phrase, a side glimpse into the human comedy. If poetry is not good, it is positively nothing.

The earliest poet of historical consequence—the only form of his poetical consequence—of the Southwest was Mirabeau Buonaparte Lamar. He led the Texas cavalry at San Jacinto, became president of the Republic of Texas, organized the futile Santa Fe Expedition, gathered up six volumes of notes and letters for a history of Texas that might have been as raw-meat realistic as anything in Zola or Tolstoy. Then as a poet he reached his climax in "The Daughter of Mendoza"—a graceful but moonshiny imitation of Tom Moore and Lord Byron. Perhaps it is better for the weak to imitate than to try to be original.

It would not take one more than an hour to read aloud all the poetry of the Southwest that could stand rereading. At the top of all I should place Fay Yauger's "Planter's Charm," published in a volume of the same title. With it belongs "The Hired Man on Horseback," by Eugene Manlove Rhodes, a long poem of passionate fidelity to his own decent kind of men, with power to ennoble the reader, and with the form necessary to all beautiful composition. This is the sole and solitary piece of poetry to be found in all the myriads of rhymes classed as "cowboy poetry." I'd want Stanley Vestal's "Fandango," in a volume of the same title. Margaret Bell Houston's "Song from the Traffic," which takes one to the feathered mesquites and the bluebonnets, might come next. Begging pardon of the perpetually palpitating New Mexico lyricists, I would skip most of them, except for bits of Mary Austin, Witter Bynner, Haniel Long, and maybe somebody I don't know, and go to George Sterling's "Father Coyote"—in California. Probably I would come back to gallant Phil LeNoir's "Finger of Billy the Kid," written while he was dying of tuberculosis in New Mexico. I wouldn't leave without the swift, brilliantly economical stanzas that open the ballad of "Sam Bass," and a single line, "He came of a solitary race," in the ballad of "Jesse James."

Several other poets have, of course, achieved something for mortals to enjoy and be lifted by. Their work has been sifted into various anthologies. The best one is *Signature of the Sun: Southwest Verse, 1900-1950*, selected and edited by Mabel Major and T. M. Pearce, University of New Mexico Press, Albuquerque, 1950. Two other anthologies are *Songs of the Cattle Trail and Cow Camp*, by John A. Lomax, 1919, reprinted in 1950 by Duell, Sloan and Pearce, New York; *The Road to Texas*, by Whitney Montgomery, Kaleidograph, Dallas, 1940. Montgomery's Kaleidograph Press has published many volumes by southwestern poets. Somebody who has read them all and has read all the poets represented, without enough of distillation, in *Signature of the Sun* could no doubt be juster on the subject than I am.

Like historical fiction, drama of the Southwest has been less dramatic than actuality and less realistic than real characters. Lynn Riggs of Oklahoma, author of *Green Grow the Lilacs*, has so far been the most successful dramatist.

34

Miscellaneous Interpreters and Institutions

ARTISTS

ART MAY BE SUBSTANTIVE, but more than being its own excuse for being, it lights up the land it depicts, shows people what is significant, cherishable in their own lives and environments. Thus Peter Hurd of New Mexico has revealed windmills, Thomas Hart Benton of Missouri has elevated mules. Nature may not literally follow art, but human eyes follow art and literature in recognizing nature.

The history of art in the Southwest, if it is ever rightly written, will not bother with the Italian "Holy Families" imported by agent-guided millionaires trying to buy exclusiveness. It will begin with clay (Indian pottery), horse hair (vaquero weaving), hide (vaquero plaiting), and horn (backwoods carving). It will note Navajo sand painting and designs in blankets.

Charles M. Russell's art has been characterized in the chapter on "Range Life." He had to paint, and the Old West was his life. More versatile was his contemporary Frederic Remington, author of *Pony Tracks, Crooked Trails,* and other books, and prolific illustrator of Owen Wister, Theodore Roosevelt, Alfred Henry Lewis, and numerous other writers of the West. Not so well known as these two, but rising in estimation, was Charles Schreyvogle. He did not write; his best-known pictures are reproduced in a folio entitled *My Bunkie and Others.* Remington, Russell, and Schreyvogle all did superb sculptoring in bronze. One of the finest pieces of sculpture in the Southwest is "The Seven Mustangs" by A. Phimister Proctor, in front of the Texas Memorial Museum at Austin.

Among contemporary artists, Ross Santee and Will James (died, 1942) have illustrated their own cow country books, some of which are listed under "Range Life" and "Horses." William R. Leigh, author of *The Western Pony,* is a significant painter of the range. Edward Borein of Santa Barbara, California, has in scores of etchings and a limited amount of book illustrations "documented" many phases of western life. Buck Dunton of Taos illustrated also. His lithographs and paintings of wild animals, trappers, cowboys, and Indians seem secure.

I cannot name and evaluate modern artists of the Southwest. They are many, and the excellence of numbers of them is nationally recognized. Many articles have been written about the artists who during this century have lived around Taos and painted that region of the Southwest. Some of the better-known names are Ernest L. Blumenschein, Oscar Berninghaus, Ward Lockwood, B. J. O. Nordfeldt, Georgia O'Keeffe, Ila McAfee, Barbara Latham Cook, Howard Cook. Artists thrive in Arizona, Oklahoma, and Texas as well as in New Mexico. Tom Lea, of El Paso, may be quitting painting and drawing to spend the remainder of his life in writing. Perhaps he himself does not know. Jerry Bywaters, who is at work on the history of art in the Southwest, has about quit producing to direct the Dallas Museum of Fine Arts. Alexandre Hogue gives his strength to teaching art in Tulsa University. Exhibitions, not commentators, are the revealers of art.

A few books, all expensive, reproduce the art of certain depicters of the West and Southwest. *Etchings of the West,* by Edward Borein, and *The West of Alfred Jacob Miller* have been noted in other chapters (consult Index). Other recent art works are: *Peter Hurd: Portfolio of Landscapes and Portraits,* University of New Mexico Press, Albuquerque, 1950; *Gallery of Western Paintings,* edited by Raymond Carlson,

McGraw-Hill, New York, 1951 (unsatisfactory reproduction); *Frederic Remington, Artist of the Old West*, by Harold McCracken, Lippincott, Philadelphia, 1947 (biography and check list with many reproductions); *Portrait of the Old West*, by Harold McCracken, McGraw-Hill, New York, 1952 (samplings of numerous artists).

In February, 1946, Robert Taft of the University of Kansas began publishing in the *Kansas Historical Quarterly* chapters, richly illustrated in black and white, in "The Pictorial Record of the Old West." The book to be made from these chapters will have a historical validity missing in most picture books.

MAGAZINES

The leading literary magazine of the region is the *Southwest Review*, published quarterly at Southern Methodist University, Dallas. The *New Mexico Quarterly*, published by the University of New Mexico at Albuquerque, the *Arizona Quarterly*, published by the University of Arizona at Tucson, the *Colorado Quarterly*, published by the University of Colorado at Boulder, and *Prairie Schooner*, University of Nebraska Press, Lincoln, are excellent exponents of current writing in the Southwest and West. All these magazines are liberated from provincialism.

HISTORICAL SOCIETIES

Every state in the Southwest has a state historical organization that publishes. The oldest and most productive of these, outside of California, is the Texas State Historical Association, with headquarters at Austin.

HISTORIES

A majority of the state histories of the Southwest have been written with the hope of securing an adoption for school use. It would require a blacksnake whip to make most juveniles, or adults either, read these productions, as devoid of picturesqueness, life-blood, and intellectual content as so many concrete slabs. No genuinely humanistic history of the Southwest has ever been printed. There are good factual histories—and a history not based on facts can't possibly be good—but the lack of synthesis, of intelligent evaluations, of imagination, of the seeing eye and portraying hand is too evident. The stuff out of which history is woven—diaries, personal narratives, county histories, chronicles of ranches and trails, etc.—has been better done than history itself.

FOLKLORE

Considered scientifically, folklore belongs to science and not to the humanities. When folk and fun are not scienced out of it, it is song and story and in literature is mingled with other ingredients of life and art, as exampled by the folklore in *Hamlet* and *A Midsummer Night's Dream.* In "Indian Culture," "Spanish-Mexican Strains," "Backwoods Life and Humor," "Cowboy Songs," "The Bad Man Tradition," "Bears," "Coyotes," "Negro Folk Songs and Tales," and other chapters of this *Guide* numerous books charged with folklore have been listed.

The most active state society of its kind in America has been the Texas Folklore Society, with headquarters at the University of Texas, Austin. Volume XXIV of its Publications appeared in 1951, and it has published and distributed other books. Its Publications are now distributed by Southern Methodist University Press in Dallas. J. Frank Dobie, with constant help, was editor from 1922 to 1943, when he resigned. Since 1943 Mody C. Boatright has been editor.

In 1947 the New Mexico Folklore Society began publishing yearly the *New Mexico Folklore Record.* It is printed by the University of New Mexico Press. The University of Arizona, Tucson, has published several folklore bulletins. The California Folklore Society publishes, through the University of California Press, Berkeley, *Western Folklore,* a quarterly.

In co-operation with the Southeastern Folklore Society, the University of Florida, Gainesville, publishes the *Southern Folklore Quarterly*. Levette J. Davidson of the University of Denver, author of *A Guide to American Folklore,* University of Denver Press, 1951, directs the Western Folklore Conference. The *Journal of American Folklore* has published a good deal from the Southwest and Mexico. The Sociedad Folklorica de Mexico publishes its own *Anurio*. Between 1929 and 1932, B. A. Botkin, editor of *A Treasury of Southern Folklore,* 1949, and *A Treasury of Western Folklore,* 1951 (Crown, New York), brought out four volumes entitled *Folk-Say,* University of Oklahoma Press. OP. The volumes are significant for literary utilizations of folklore and interpretations of folks.

MUSEUMS

Museums do not belong to the DAR. Their perspective on the past is constructive. The growing museums in Santa Fe, Tucson, Phoenix, Tulsa, Oklahoma City, Houston, San Antonio, Dallas, Austin, Denver, and on west into California represent the art, fauna, flora, geology, archeology, occupations, transportation, architecture, and other phases of the Southwest in a way that may be more informing than many printed volumes.

35

Subjects for Themes

THE OBJECT OF THEME-WRITING is to make a student observe, to become aware, to evaluate, to enrich himself. Any phase of life or literature named or suggested in the foregoing chapters could be taken as a subject for an essay. The most immature essay must be more than a summary; a mere summary is never an essay. The writer must synthesize, make his own combination of thoughts, facts, incidents, characteristics, anecdotes, interpretations, illustrations, according to his own pattern. A writer is a weaver, weaving various threads of various hues and textures into a design that is his own.

"Look into thy heart and write." "Write what you know about." All this is good advice in a way — but students have to write themes whether they have anything to write or not. The way to get full of a subject, to generate a conveyable interest, is to fill up on the subject. As clouds are but transient forms of matter that "change but cannot die," so most writing, even the best, is but a variation in form of experiences, ideas, observations, emotions that have been recorded over and over.

In general, the materials a student weaves are derived from three sources: what he has read, what he has heard, what he has observed and experienced himself. If he chooses to sketch an interesting character, he will make his sketch richer and more interesting if he reads all he can find that illuminates his subject's background. If he sets out to tell a legend or a series of related folk tales or anecdotes, he will improve his telling by reading what he can on the subjects that his proposed narratives treat of and by reading similar narratives already written by others. If he wishes to tell what he knows about rattlesnakes, buzzards, pet coyotes, Brahma cattle, prickly pear, cottonwoods, Caddo Lake, the Brazos River, Santa Fe adobes, or other features of the land, let him bolster and put into perspective his own knowledge by reading what others have said on the matter. Knowledge fosters originality. Reading gives ideas.

The list of subjects that follows is meant to be suggestive, and must not be regarded as inclusive. The best subject for any writer is one that he is interested in. A single name or category may afford scores of subjects. For example, take Andy Adams, the writer about cowboys and range life. His campfire yarns, the attitude of his cowboys toward their horses, what he has to say about cows, the metaphor of the range as he has recorded it, the placidity of his cowboys as opposed to Zane Grey sensationalism, etc., are a few of the subjects to be derived from a study of his books. Or take a category like "How the Early Settlers Lived." Pioneer food, transportation, sociables, houses, neighborliness, loneliness, living on game meat, etc., make subjects. Almost every subject listed below will suggest either variations or associated subjects.

The Humor of the Southwest

Similes from Nature (Crockett is rich in them)

The Code of Individualism

The Code of the Range

Six-shooter Ethics

The Right to Kill

The Tradition of Cowboy Gallantry (read Owen Wister's *The Virginian* and *A Journey in Search of Christmas;* also novels by Eugene Manlove Rhodes)

Frontier Hospitality

Amusements (shooting matches, tournaments, play parties, dances, poker, horse races, quiltings, house-raisings)

The Western Gambler (Bret Harte and Alfred Henry Lewis have idealized him in fiction; he might be contrasted with the Mississippi River gambler)

Indian Captives

The Age of Horse Culture (Spanish, Indian, Anglo-American; the horse was important enough to any one of these classes to warrant extended study)

The Cowboy's Horse

The Cowboy Myth (Mody Boatright is writing a book on the subject)

Evolution of the Frontier Criminal Lawyer

The Frontier Intellect in the Atomic Age

British Chroniclers of the West

Civilized Perspective in Writings on the Old West

The Indian in Fiction

Fictional Betrayal of the West

The West in Reality and the West on the Screen

Around the Chuck Wagon: Cowboy Yarns

Stretching the Blanket

Authentic Liars

Recent Fiction of the Southwest (any writer worth writing about)

Literary Magazines of the Southwest

Ranch Women

Mexican Labor (on ranch, farm, or in town)

Mexican Folk Tales

Backwoods Life in Frederick Gerstaecker

"The Old Cattleman" in Alfred Henry Lewis' *Wolfville* Books

Mayne Reid as an Exponent of the Southwest (see estimate of him in *Mesa, Cañon and Pueblo,* by Charles F. Lummis)

The Gunman in Fiction and Reality (O. Henry, Bret Harte, Alfred Henry Lewis; *The Saga of Billy the Kid,* by Walter Noble Burns; Gillett's *Six Years with the Texas Rangers;* Webb's *The Texas Rangers;* Lake's *Wyatt Earp*)

Character of the Trail Drivers

Cowboy's Life as Reflected in His Songs

"Wrathy to Kill a Bear" (the frontiersman as a destroyer of wild life)

"I Thought I Might See Something to Shoot at"

Anecdotes of the Stump Speaker

Exempla of Revivalists and Campmeeting Preachers

The Campmeeting

Stagecoaching

Life on the Santa Fe Trail

The Rendezvous of the Mountain Men

In the Covered Wagon

Squatter Life

No Shade

From Grass to Wheat

From Wheat to Dust

Brush (a special study of prickly pear, the mesquite, or some other form of flora could be made)

Cotton (whole books are suggested here, the tenant farmer being one of the subjects)

Oil Booms

Longhorns

Coyote Stories

Deer Nature, or Whitetails and Their Hunters

Rattlesnakes, or Rattlesnake Stories

Panther Stories

Tarantula Lore

Grasshopper Plagues

The Javelina in Fact and in Folk Tale

The Roadrunner (Paisano)

Wild Turkeys

The Poisoned-Out Prairie Dog

Sheep

Vanishing Sheep Herders

The Bee Hunter

Pot Hunters

Buffalo Hunters
The Bar Hunter and Bar Stories
Indian Fighter
Indian Hater
Scalps
Squaw Men
Mountain Men and Grizzlies
Scouts and Guides
Stage Drivers
Fiddlers and Fiddle Tunes
Frontier Justices of the Peace
 (Roy Bean set the example)
Horse Traders
Horse Racers
Newspapermen
Frontier Schoolteacher
Circuit Rider
Pony Express Rider
Folk Tales of My Community
Flavorsome Characters of My Community
Stanley Vestal
Harvey Fergusson
Kansas Cow Towns
Drought and Thirst
Washington Irving on the West

Witty Repartee in Eugene Manlove
 Rhodes
Bigfoot Wallace's Humor
Charles M. Russell as Artist of the
 West (or any other western
 artist)
Learning to See Life Around Me
Features of My Own Cultural
 Inheritance
I Heard It Back Home
Family Traditions
My Family's Interesting Character
Doodlebugs in the Sand
Bobwhites
Blue Quail
Coachwhips and Other Good Snakes
Mockingbird Habits
Jack Rabbit Lore
Catfish Lore
Herb Remedies
"Criticism of Life" in Southwestern
 Fiction
Intellectual Integrity in_____
 (Name of writer or writers or
 some locally prominent news-
 paper to be supplied)

Index